T0156957

SAVED, NOW WHAT?

written by
Tara Jones

Order this book online at www.trafford.com
or email orders@trafford.com

Most Trafford titles are also available at major online book retailers.

Printed in the United States of America.

ISBN: 978-1-4669-1022-5 (sc)
ISBN: 978-1-4669-1024-9 (hc)
ISBN: 978-1-4669-1023-2 (e)

Library of Congress Control Number: 2012904992

Trafford rev. 02/27/2012

 www.trafford.com

North America & international
toll-free: 1 888 232 4444 (USA & Canada)
phone: 250 383 6864 ♦ fax: 812 355 4082

THIS BOOK IS DEDICATED

TO MY MOM AND SON

FOR LOVING ME THROUGH IT ALL!

CONTENTS

PREFACE

Hello, my name is Tara and I profess to be a Christian (follower of Jesus Christ). I am not perfect by any means and writing this book does not make me an "expert", but just a vessel (a hollow receptacle capable of holding substance). What I have learned over the years, I think it's time for me to share it with my brothers and sisters in Christ. I tried to make this the third book I published. I wanted to publish the two kid books I wrote first, but for almost 2 years I have been trying to get illustrations done. I tried to get my illustrations done by a family member, he was a published illustrator. He dragged it on for months and finally when he said he had them ready, he didn't show up to bring them to me or respond to text or calls. Next, a young lady said she would be able to do my illustrations. After weeks of me thinking she was working on my illustrations she stated she didn't have time to work on the project. I then tried several more people to get my illustrations done. They would take on the project but then after a few weeks to a few months stated they were unable to complete the illustrations for one reason or another.

I was literally upset & angry, because I thought these kid books needed to be published. I thought they were positive & wholesome books that would teach kids about love, family values and sharing. I love kids and I wanted to bless them through my books. I didn't get a revelation (the act of revealing a divine truth) that God was blocking the other books, because He wanted me to focus on this book and get this book published first.

So, now I am handling my assignment and it is actually past due. I believe we are on this earth for a reason. If something bothers you in your spirit then help find a solution. Where there is a problem, be a problem solver instead of being part of the problem. A lot of times we can talk a big game about things not being done or accomplished, but what are we doing about it? I really had an issue about knowing what comes next after being saved. Just like getting married, everybody prepares for the wedding, but what about after the wedding. After you have spent all that money on the food, decorations, the tuxedo & the wedding dress (looking wonderful), but what about after the wedding, after you have spent all that money, your friends have went home, after the honeymoon and you have said all those beautiful words to each other in front of God, the Pastor, your friends and family. What happens after the first set of bills come in, the first time a check bounces, the first time one of your in-laws ask to move in and the list goes on and on.

The solution is to talk to someone that has wisdom, knowledge.

Proverbs 23:23 says, "Buy the truth and do not sell it; get wisdom, discipline and understanding.

Talk to someone that has been through that same situation or has knowledge of that subject. It's great to get counseling or guidance. I am not an expert, but with God's word I can give you some basics. You should always study God's word for yourself, always listen to wisdom. I know we don't want to be wrong and sometimes we want to contest when someone is telling us something that is right.

Proverbs 11:2 says, when pride comes, then comes disgrace; but with humility comes wisdom.

I used to be so prideful and didn't want to take any advice I didn't agree with, but it is not about me, it is about getting it right in God's eyes. Remember when we were younger and our parents used to tell us what to do. You know all those rules and we just were not trying to hear that—too many rules. You ever heard this line from your parents, "a hard head makes a soft behind". Meaning if you keep misbehaving you would get a spanking or if you continue to go against the rules you will have to deal with the consequences. So, it is best to be a good kid, which I know when you get to a certain age, we think we are too grown for rules. But, it doesn't matter what age you are, we all have to obey rules and if you are a Christian you are a child of God and He wants you to be a good child-amen.

Throughout this book I will tell you some things about me and just everyday life, but connect it to the word of God. Please know that this book was created because I wanted to be a vessel, a witness, to help others and obey my assignment.

I want you to know it is more to just saying I am a Christian. It's about touching lives, bringing others to Christ and sharing your gifts and talents. Also, growing in Christ until the day he returns. You will find out that a lot of times there is something missing in our lives and it is in the word of God. He has so much for us. We are His children and He loves us and wants what is best for us. He also wants us to go beyond just being saved! Amen

CHAPTER 1

"HOW DID I GET HERE?"

When I decided to be a Christian I was not in church, I was invited to a weekend retreat that a co-worker's church was hosting. I had been enjoying my so called life going from relationship to relationship, which included friendships. I was always laughing to keep from crying, the life of the party. I was looking for someone to love me and to fill the empty void I had, not knowing I was missing God.

I remember an annoying girl at my job. She came to work on a daily basis talking about Jesus and her church from the time she got to work until she went home, well in between calls we worked in a call center. She got on my last nerve, but that's because I had a carnal mind (wordly-not thinking on spiritual things) and she was doing what she was assigned to do as a Christian. She was witnessing (a person who gives testimony, testifies).

John 1:6-8 says, There came a man who was sent from God; his name was John. He came as a witness to testify concerning that light, he came only as a witness to the light. The true light that gives light to every man was coming into the world.

She was witnessing to me, telling me what she had learned about Jesus Christ and that I need to get my life in order, but I didn't listen until one day I was in need and my friends couldn't help me, but guess what she did and that changed my whole mindset about her. So, when she asked me to the retreat I said, "yes". The retreat was from Friday through Sunday, the location was at a Holiday Inn and the First Lady (which is what some people call their Pastor's wife) and some of the women of the church got a suite. When I arrived they were all at the indoor pool and I was scared because I didn't know any of them, but they treated me just like a sister. I didn't have a swimsuit and someone let me borrow theirs. Over the course of the weekend we were swimming, laughing, joking getting to know each other, but late at night that is when it got deep. The first lady was talking to the ladies about their issues and answering their questions. I had never experienced someone of such wisdom giving her time like that, to listen and respond to others needs. As I listened I realized I was where I needed to be "period", it came over me that my life was going nowhere, no purpose. I went to sleep with questions on my mind and the real question was, "if I died tonight, where would I go-to hell or heaven?" I couldn't be for sure. Needless to say I was saved that Sunday morning.

I've always known something was missing from my life since I was little girl. I felt out of place, looking for something, but didn't exactly know what. My mom took me to church sometimes as a child. I remember falling asleep in her lap listening to the preacher screaming and yelling about something that I didn't understand. I guess some of the adults didn't understand either, because some of them were sleep too. I went to vacation bible school sometimes and learned even less.

I remember as a pre-teen, our neighbor was asking all the little kids in the neighborhood to come to her house for bible study, my mom said it was ok for me to go. The lady gave us all a little red book, I knew how the bible looked and this was not one. When she was teaching my spirit was not connecting with it, this carried on for a few weeks. I went home and told my mom what she was teaching us and showed her the book. My mom said it was not the bible and it was of some other religion and she told me to stop attending the bible studies and return the book. That goes to show you to find out all information before agreeing to participate. I am not against anyone else's religion, because everyone thinks their religion is the right one. I just choose to be a Christian, I believe God chose me to be one of his children and I am grateful.

John 10:27-28: my sheep listen to my voice; I know them and they follow me. I give them eternal life and they shall never perish; no one can snatch them out of my hand.

God knew us before we were born and all the mistakes we would make, but that does not stop him from loving us and being our Father.

Jeremiah 1:5—"Before I formed you in the womb I knew you, before you were born I set you apart; I appointed you as a prophet to the nations."

God chose you: **Eph 1:4-5** says, Long ago even before He made the world, God loved us and chose us in Christ to be holy without fault in his eyes. His unchanging plan has always been to adopt us into his own family by bringing us to himself through Jesus Christ and this gave Him great pleasure.

CHAPTER 2

"CONFESSION"

However you came to Christ, through a friend, co-worker, stranger, enemy, at a concert or watching television. It doesn't matter, what matters is you did once you made your heart and mind up. You believed that God's son Jesus Christ died for your sins and rose again and is alive today. The moment you pray and ask Jesus Christ to forgive your sins, He will.

1 John 1:9—If we confess our sins, He is faithful and just and will forgive us our sins and cleanse us from every wrong.

Romans 10:9—If you confess that Jesus is your Lord and you believe in your heart that God raised Him from the dead, you will be saved.

Now, you have been saved by God's free grace.

Eph 2:8-10: For it is by grace you have been saved, through faith and this not from yourselves, it is the gift of God-not by works, so that no one can boast. For we are God's workmanship, created in Christ Jesus to do good works, which God prepared in advance for us to do.

When someone gives you a gift, what do you say? The appropriate response would be to say, 'thank you", often Christians even after they have been given the gift of salvation, they feel obligated to try to work their way to God. Because our salvation and even our faith are gifts, we should respond with gratitude, joy and praise. We become Christians through God's unmerited grace not as the result of any effort, ability, intelligent choice or act of service on our part.

However, out of gratitude for this free gift, we will seek to help and serve others through kindness, love and gentleness and not merely to please ourselves. While no action or work we do can help us obtain salvation. God's intention is that our salvation will result in acts of service. We are not saved merely to our own benefit but to serve Christ and build up the church.

We are God's workmanship, our salvation is something only God can do. It is his powerful, creative work in us. If God considers us his works of art, we dare not treat ourselves or others with any disrespect or as inferior work.

We are saved solely on what Jesus Christ has already done for us. Our connection with God is through His Son.

Romans 5:8-God demonstrated His love for us in that while we were still separated from God by sin, Christ died for us.

If you have never experienced, or heard the story of Jesus Christ's life and death. I recommend "The Passion of Christ". It is very close to the bible description that I have seen in my Christian life (**read Luke chapters 23-24 prior to watching**). Please adults look at the movie alone without your children when you make your own determination when and if you want your kids to watch it. There are always animated movies on their level they can watch (Mardel's Christian bookstore has a large selection).

I went to see the "Passion of Christ" at the movie theatre when it first came out years ago. I cried so hard I could hardly breathe. My heart was breaking and my spirit was in pain from seeing what Jesus actually went through to save our souls.

John 3:16-17: For God so loved the world that He gave his only begotten Son, so that everyone who believes in Him will not perish, but have eternal life. God did not send his son into the world to condemn it, but save it.

Remember the old saying, "confession is good for the soul." That has proved to be the truth. Amen

CHAPTER 3

"BAPTISM"

Usually, after you make the wonderful decision to be a Christian then there is baptizing or baptism. Baptize means to dip under water or be immersed in water. Baptism symbolizes the death and resurrection of Christ. It is a celebration that you can share with your friends and family. Baptism is usually done during a church service. You will be told by your minister what to do. It is really simple. If you are baptized in a church baptismal tank (sometimes called baptismal pool), it is filled with warm water before you arrive. Both you and the minister step into the water (unless it is a smaller, portable baptismal tank the minister maybe on the outside and you on the inside). To prevent the water from entering your mouth or nose, you should keep your mouth closed and hold your nose (depending on how the minister instructs you). The minister will place one hand on your back and the other on your hand or arm. You will be lowered into the water back first and then quickly lifted up. It takes only a few seconds. Water baptism is very exciting! It is celebration for all to see. You have accepted Jesus as your Savior and He has forgiven your sins. Now, you have publicly shown your decision! You are a new person!

1 Cor 15:3-4: Christ died for our sins just as the scriptures said. He was buried and raised from the dead on the third day as the scriptures said.

Col 2:12: For when you are baptized, you were buried with Christ and in baptism you were also raised with Christ.

So, when you go down in the water that represents death (old man—meaning the old person you used to be). When you are brought back up out of the water that represents when Christ rose from the dead (the new man-new life).

We are just following the way Jesus was baptized in the Bible.

Matt 3:16-17: After His baptism, Jesus came up out of the water, the Heavens were opened and He saw the spirit of God descended like a dove and settled on him and a voice from the Heavens said, "This is my beloved son and I am fully pleased with Him."

I am sure God is pleased with you too after your baptism.

Romans 6:4—For we died and were buried with Christ by baptism and just as Christ was raised from the dead by the glorious power of the Father. Now, we also may live new lives.

2 Cor 5:17—When someone becomes a Christian, he becomes a brand new person inside. The old life has passed away and a new life has begun.

Now, remember baptism does not make a believer—it shows that you already believe. Also, baptism does not "save" you only your faith in Christ does that. Baptism symbolizes the commitment you made in your heart.

Acts 8:12—But, now the people believed Philip's message of the Good news concerning the Kingdom of God and the name of Jesus Christ. As result many men & women were baptized.

Acts 2:38-41: Those who believed and accepted his message were baptized.

Do you have to be baptized to go to Heaven? Not at all. The best proof we have is when the thief who hung on the cross next to Jesus when He was crucified. This criminal believed Jesus was the Son of God and asked Him for forgiveness. Jesus told him that he would go to Paradise that day.

Luke 23:39-43: One of the criminals who hung there hurled insults at him: "Aren't you the Christ? Save yourself and us!" But the other criminal rebuked him, "Don't you fear God, he said, since you are under the same sentence?" We are punished justly, for we are getting what our deeds deserve. But this man has done nothing wrong." Then he said, "Jesus, remember me when you come into your kingdom." Jesus answered, "I tell you the truth, today you will be with me in paradise.

Being baptized is part of the "Great Commission" given by Jesus.

Matt 28:18-20 says, Jesus came and told his disciples, "I have been given complete authority in heaven and on earth. Therefore, go and make disciples of all nations, baptizing them in the name of the Father and the Son and the Holy Spirit. Teach these new disciples to obey all the commands I have given you. And be sure of this: I am with you always, even to the end of time."

I remember my baptism quite well. It was me, the pastor and assistant pastor in the baptismal pool. When they were about to take me under the water, the assistant pastor said, "You may need to dunk her twice!" I was taken under with my eyes wide like a deer in headlights based on being surprised by the remark. But it was all in fun and I know he said that since I came to their church with my very funny side and was always making jokes. When I came up out the water (which I was just dipped once), the whole church was praising God for my decision. That was one of the happiest days of my life. I pray that your baptism will be one of the happiest days of your life. Amen

CHAPTER 4

"THE LORD'S SUPPER"

The Lord's Supper is sometimes called "communion". It is usually done on the first Sunday of each month at church. This is based on the order of your church you attend. You may walk around to the alter or the ushers or deacons will bring them to you. You will receive a cracker or wafer (which represents the bread in the bible scripture which also represents Jesus body) and you will receive a small tiny cup of grape juice (which represents the wine in the bible scripture which also represents Jesus blood that was shed for our sins). Once everyone receives it, usually the Pastor or Bishop of the church will pray based on the scripture in the Bible pertaining to the "Lord's last supper". Eating the bread and drinking the cup shows that we are remembering Christ's death for us and renewing our commitment to serve Him.

Luke 22:14-30: When the hour came, Jesus and his apostles reclined at the table. And He said to them, "I have eagerly desired to eat this Passover with you before I suffer. For I tell you, I will not eat it again until it finds fulfillment in the kingdom of God." After taking the cup, He gave thanks and said, "Take this and divide it among you. For I tell you I will not drink again of the fruit of the vine until the kingdom of God comes." And He took bread, gave thanks and broke it, and gave it to them, saying, "This is my body given for you; do this in remembrance of me." In the same way, after the supper He took the cup, saying, "This cup is the new covenant in my blood, which is poured out for you.

1 Cor 11:23-26: For I received from the Lord what I also passed on to you: The Lord Jesus, on the night He was betrayed, took bread, and when He had given thanks, he broke it and said, "This is my body, which is for you; do this in remembrance of me." In the same way, after supper He took the cup, saying, "This cup is the new covenant in my blood; do this, whenever you drink it, in remembrance of me." For whenever you eat this bread and drink this cup, you proclaim the Lord's death until He comes.

Before you take the Lord's Supper please examine yourself.

1 Cor 11:27-34: Therefore, whoever eats the bread or drinks the cup of the Lord in an unworthy manner will be guilty of sinning against the body and blood of the Lord. A man ought to examine himself before he eats of the bread and drinks of the cup. For anyone who eats and drinks without recognizing the body of the Lord eats and drinks judgment on himself. That is why many among you are weak and sick, and a number of you have fallen asleep. But if we judged ourselves, we are being disciplined, so that we will not be condemned with the world. So then, my brothers, when you come together to eat, wait for each other. If anyone is hungry, he should eat at home, so that when you meet together it may not result in judgment.

Paul gives specific instructions on how the Lord's Supper should be observed. We should take the Lord's Supper thoughtfully because we are proclaiming that Christ died for our sins. We should take it worthily with due reverence and respect. We should examine ourselves for any un-confessed sin or resentful attitude. We are to be properly prepared based on our belief in and love for Christ. We should be considerate of others waiting until everyone is there and then eating in an orderly and unified manner.

When Paul said that no one should take the Lord's Supper in an unworthy manner, he was speaking to the church members who were rushing into it without thinking of its meaning. Those who did so were "guilty of sinning against the body and blood of the Lord." Instead of honoring his sacrifice, they were sharing in the guilt of those who crucified Christ. In reality, no one is worthy to take the Lord's Supper. We are all sinners saved by grace. This is why we should prepare ourselves for Communion through confession of sin and resolution of differences with others. These actions remove the barriers that affect our relationship with Christ and with other believers. Awareness of your sin should not keep you away from Communion but should drive you to participate in it.

"Without recognizing the body of the Lord" means not understanding what the Lord's Supper means and not distinguishing it from a normal meal. Those who do so condemn themselves.

Fallen asleep is another way of describing death. That some of the people had died may have been a special supernatural judgment on the Corinthian church. This type of disciplinary judgment highlights the seriousness of the Communion service. The Lord's Supper is not to be taken lightly; this new covenant cost Jesus his life. It is not a meaningless ritual, but a sacrament given by Christ to help strengthen our faith.

People should come to this meal desiring to fellowship with other believers and prepare for the Lord's Supper to follow, not to fill upon a big dinner. "If anyone is hungry, he should eat at home" means that they should eat dinner beforehand, so as to come to the fellowship meal in the right frame of mind.

To me this is very serious and important time to remember what Jesus sacrificed for us. He gave himself fully and unselfishly.

Communion can also be done with your family at home, if you would like. I am saying in addition to church communion together with your church family. The bible did not say once a month, it says, "as often as you do this-do this in remembrance of me." Jesus is so worthy and communion helps us to remember how much.

CHAPTER 5

"THE BIBLE"

The bible is a book that consists of writings inspired by God. God spoke to several people over many years and told them what to write. Over time, these writings were gathered together and put in one book we call the bible today. The bible consists of 66 books, 39 in the Old Testament and 27 in the New Testament. Each book is divided into chapters and each chapter is divided into verses. A bible is your sword against evil, things that come against you.

If you don't already own a bible, you need to get one. And even if you do own a bible, you may need to get one that is easy to understand. Jesus didn't speak using a lot of "thee's and thou's" so don't feel you have to use a bible that's filled with a lot of weird-looking words.

Two bible versions that are pretty easy to understand are the New International Version (NIV) and the New Living Translation (NLT). There's even a version for younger readers or people who have trouble reading called the New International Reader's Version (NirV).

Another thing to think about when choosing a bible is whether you want one that has study notes in it. Some bibles have footnotes to help you understand and apply what you read, and others are just the bible and nothing else. Both the Life Application Bible and the Full Life Study Bible in the New International Version are easy versions to read, and the notes have very practical ways to help you apply what you read.

Once you have a Bible, you need to spend some time checking out how it's put together. The Bible is divided into two parts: the Old Testament, which was written before Jesus was born and the New Testament, which was written after Jesus was born. Each part or testament is divided into books, and each book is divided into chapters and verses. It's helpful to get to know the names of the books of the Bible so you can find them more easily, but there's a table of contents in the front of the Bible if you need help.

You can purchase a bible at your local Mardel's Christian bookstore (or your nearby Christian bookstore), they have such a wonderful selection of bibles for any need meaning: adult, new Christian, easy reader, kids, pre-teens, college bound etc. I don't know if they still do it or not, but the last time I was there with a purchase of a bible they engraved my name on it for free, I can't guarantee they still do that.

Now it's time to start reading. Most Christians think the New Testament is easier to understand than most of the Old Testament books, so it's easier to start there. The first four books of the New Testament were written by four different men-Matthew, Mark, Luke, and John, and they each tell the story of Jesus' life on earth. The next book, Acts, tells the story of the first Christians. The rest of the New Testament (except for the last book, Revelation) contains letters that different men wrote to the churches that were around at that time. Revelation talks about what's going to happen in the future.

So what should you read first? Reading about Jesus' life on earth is a good place to start. Seeing how He acted and treated people while He was here will help you understand what He wants you to do. Mark is a good place to begin.

Psalms and Proverbs are books in the Old Testament that are easy to understand and you can start reading those, too. Psalms is a book of 150 songs that cover every kind of emotion you can imagine-love, hate, anger, revenge, and joy. Many of the Psalms are praises to God for His blessings.

The book of Proverbs is filled with short, wise sayings about how you should live. You hear proverbs every day, such as, "Early to bed, early to rise, make a man healthy, wealthy, and wise," or "A bird in the hand is worth two in the bush." These are not in the Bible, but the Proverbs in the Bible are filled with even better advice like, "Lazy hands make a man poor, but diligent hands bring wealth" (**Proverbs 10:4**)

Reading the bible is the best way to know what God is saying to you. The bible is called God's word and that's exactly what it is-kind of like a letter God has written to you. By reading the bible, you'll discover how wonderful God is and how much He loves you. You'll also get instructions from Him on how to live your life.

The word of God is your protection filled with wisdom and knowledge, which will direct your path.

Hebrews 4:12-13: For the word of God is full of living power. It is sharper than a two edge sword, cutting deep into our inter-most thoughts and desires. It exposes us for what we really are. Nothing in all creation can hide from Him, everything is naked and exposed before his eyes. This is the God to whom we must explain all that we have done.

That is why when the Pastor is teaching, you are thinking how did he know all of my business and sometimes getting mad, but he is only giving you the word of God which reveals all.

Eph 6:17—Put on salvation helmet and take the sword of the spirit which is the word of God.

2 Tim 3:16—All scripture is inspired by God and is useful to teach us what is true and to make us realize what is wrong in our lives. It straightens us out and teaches us to do what is right. It is God's way of preparing us in every way, fully equipped for every good thing God wants us to do.

Read your bible the word of God, so you can know scriptures and use them in your daily lives. **Matt 22:29**—Jesus replied, "Your problem is that you don't know the scriptures and you don't know the power of God.

How often should we read the bible? We should meditate on the word day and night.

Joshua 1:8-The book of the law shall not depart out of thy mouth. Meditate on it day and night. So, that you may be careful to do everything written in it. Then you will be prosperous and successful. Many people think that prosperity and success come from having power, influential personal contacts and a relentless desire to get ahead. But the strategy for gaining prosperity that God taught Joshua goes against such criteria he said that to succeed Joshua must be strong and courageous because the task ahead would not be easy. Obey God's law-God's word. To be successful, follow God's word. You may not succeed by the world's standards, but you will be a success in God's eyes and His opinion lasts forever.

You probably want to start with the New Testament and read a chapter a day or more. Also, try to read one chapter of Psalms and Proverbs per day. You can also find studying tools at the Christian bookstore, to help you understand and read the Bible on a daily basis.

Some days you won't read that much because God will cause a verse to be really meaningful to you, and you will want to give it some thought. That's fine. You're trying to hear what God is saying, not win a race, and He doesn't keep a scoreboard up in Heaven keeping track of all the verses you have read. So, don't be hard on yourself!

The Bible has so much for you to learn. I have been a Christian for over ten years and I am still learning new things from the word of God. Please know distractions will come when you are trying to study the word of God, which includes: sleepiness, phone calls, family, relationships and television is among the top five.

Stay focus, allot yourself some time to read your bible each day. Maybe you need to read it early while household is sleep to get your day started and or at night after everyone is sleep. You also want to read the bible with your family, even if you have bible studies with your family, please don't forsake going to church. Amen!

God bless you and enjoy the word of God, because it will help you in your daily life!

CHAPTER 6

"FAITH"

You have to have faith as a Christian it is the essence of believing. When we were children we believed almost anything, the cartoons, the tooth fairy, santa clause (I do apologize if you still believe in them-amen). We believed we could be whatever we wanted to be, doctor, lawyer, the president, or a super hero. We believed until someone put doubt in our mind or told us we couldn't do it or it wasn't true. But never let anyone make you lose faith or turn to an unbeliever. It just takes a little faith to do great things. Jesus had faith, He believed in the word of God and He walked by faith and not by sight. Things might look one way, but faith will bring you through and out the other side.

After one is born again (saved), your next step is developing your faith. God is pleased when He sees us living by faith. Every step of Christian life is a faith walk.

What is faith? It is the confident assurance that what we hope for is going to happen. It is the evidence of things we can't see. God gave his approval to people in days of old because of their faith. (Read the entirety of **Hebrews chapter 11**—it gives great examples of faith stories in the bible)

Hab 2:4—But the just should live by faith. We as Christians must trust that God is directing all things according to His purposes.

2 Cor 5:7—For we walk by faith and not by sight.

Rom 12:3—God has given everyone a measure of faith

I know you may be thinking you might not have enough faith, but it doesn't take much to do great things as said above in scripture. God gives us all a measure of faith and we can build from there. Your faith is yours and you need your faith to believe in things that you need. Your faith is personal with believing in Jesus Christ and the things of Heaven and the Bible and on and on.

Luke 17:5-6 says, One day the apostles said to the Lord, "We need more faith; tell us how to get it?" Even if you had faith as small as a mustard seed," The Lord answered, "you could say to the mulberry tree, "May God up-root you and throw you into the sea." And it would obey you!

Jesus heals in response to faith: **Mark 5:27-34** says, She heard about Jesus, so she came up behind him through the crowd and touched the fringe of his robe. For she thought to herself, "If I can just touch his clothing, I will be healed." Immediately the bleeding stopped, and she could feel that she had been healed! Jesus realized at once that healing power had gone out from him, so he turned around in the crowds and asked, "Who touched my clothes?" His disciples said to him, "All this crowd is pressing around you. How can you ask, "Who touched me?" But he kept on looking around to see who had done it. Then the frightened woman, trembling at the realization of what had happened to her, came and fell at his feet and told him, what she had done. And he said to her, "Daughter, your faith has made you well. Go in peace. You have been healed."

Jesus calms the storm: **Mark 4:35-41** says, As evening came Jesus said to his disciples, "Let's cross to the other side of the lake." He was already in the boat, so they started out, leaving the crowds behind (although other boats followed). But soon a fierce storm arose. High waves began to break into the boat until it was nearly full of water. Jesus was sleeping at the back of the boat with his head on a cushion. Frantically they woke him up, shouting, "Teacher, don't you even care that we are going to drown?"

When he woke up he rebuked the wind and said to the water, "Quiet down!" Suddenly the wind stopped, and there was a great calm. And he asked them, "Why are you so afraid? Do you still not have faith in me?"

If you have faith in God and believe His word He will bless you. **Gen 15:6** says, And Abraham believed the Lord and the Lord declared him righteous, because of his faith. God calls us righteous because we have faith He exists and believe in His word.

Though he knew that he was too old to be a father at the age of 100 and Sarah, his wife, had never been able to have children. Abraham never wavered in believing God's promise. In fact, his faith grew stronger and in this he brought glory to God. He was absolutely convinced that God was able to do anything he promised and because Abraham's faith God declared him to be righteous-wasn't just for Abraham's benefit, it was for us too. Assuring us that God will also declare us to be righteous. Believe in God, who brought Jesus our Lord back from the dead. He was raised from the dead to make us right with God.

Having faith includes thinking and speaking positive. Not doubting, not to say doubt will not come to your mind, but once it does replace it with faith. Go to the word of God when in doubt or just to keep your faith!

When I go to church, I take notes and when something comes up in my life that I need to refer back to it-I just get my notes. Sometimes if I am not around my notes and I need a word for a issue I am going through at that moment, the Holy Spirit will bring the word back to my remembrance. Just like something I heard my Bishop say in a sermon or some wisdom that was given to me in the past!

Your faith will be tested from time to time, from bills to family to health etc. remember all you have learned from the word of God and by faith you can be healed and succeed!

CHAPTER 7

"THE HOLY SPIRIT"

The Holy Spirit is part of the trinity, God (The Father), Jesus (The Son) and the Holy Spirit (The Counselor and Comforter). Trinity means three- it's easier to say than the three names each time. We are not worshipping three Gods. God consists of all three. I know it is confusing and even harder to explain, but I am going to try to the best of my ability with God's word. I have learned so much from The Bishop that resides at the church I attend. In bible study if I ask him a question he will explain it until you understand, even if it may take up the whole bible study. But, please believe me you will understand and know the answer when you leave and that is how I want it to be when you read this book at least know the basics and become a part of a church that will help you continue your education of the Bible and what you want to know and the more you know the more you grow. Well, let me continue on the subject of the 'Holy Spirit'. To give an illustration of the Holy Spirit as consisting of three, just like an egg consists of the shell, the white and the yolk. It has to be broken to be revealed. Even though it consists of all three, it is 3 in 1-but it is still an egg. Even more confused, "sorry"—let's go to the word. The bible shows us that all three are real because the Bible tells us in **Matt 3:13-17**, says When Jesus was baptized in water all three were present. Jesus was standing in the water; God spoke in an audible voice from Heaven saying, "This is my son, whom

I love; with him I am well pleased," and the spirit of God (Holy Spirit) came down in the form of a dove and settling on him.

Everyone there witnessed this wonderful trinity. The Holy Spirit sometimes referred as "Holy Ghost", but it is not a ghost like Casper, there's no need to be afraid.

Jesus promises the Holy Spirit since He was going back to Heaven with the Father. He wanted to make sure that the Comforter was left with us.

Luke 24:44-49, says Then he said, "When I was with you before, I told you that everything written about me by Moses and the prophets and in the Psalms must all come true." Then he opened their minds to understand these many scriptures. And he said, "Yes, it was written long ago that the Messiah must suffer and die and rise again from the dead on the third day. With my authority, take this message of repentance to all the nations, beginning in Jerusalem: "There is forgiveness of sins for all who turn to me." You are witnesses of all these things. "And now I will send the Holy Spirit, just as my Father promised. But stay here in the city until the Holy Spirit comes and fills you with power from heaven."

Jesus opened these people's minds to understand the scriptures. The Holy Spirit does this in our lives today when we study the Bible. Sometimes when you read a passage and you don't understand you read the surrounding passages to try to get an understanding, consult others, but pray that the Holy Spirit will open your mind to understand to give you needed insight to put God's Word into action in your life.

Jesus explains the spiritual rebirth through the Holy Spirit: **John 3:3-7** says, Jesus replied, "I assure you, unless you are born again," you can never see the Kingdom of God." "What do you mean?" exclaimed Nicodemus. "How can an old man go back into his mother's womb and be born again?" Jesus replied, "The truth is, no one can enter the Kingdom of God without being born of water and the spirit. Humans can reproduce only human life, but the Holy Spirit gives new life from heaven. So, don't be surprised at my statement that you must be born again. Jesus was explaining the entrance of the Kingdom of God required repentance and spiritual rebirth. Jesus later taught that God's Kingdom has already begun in the hearts of believers, water and the spirit could refer to (1) the contrast between physical birth (water) and spiritual birth (spirit) or (2) being regenerated by the spirit and signifying that rebirth by Christian baptism. The water may also represent the cleansing action of God's Holy Spirit. Jesus was explaining the importance of a spiritual rebirth, saying that people don't enter the Kingdom by living a better life, but by being spiritually reborn.

God became a man in Jesus so that Jesus could die for our sins. Jesus rose from the dead to offer salvation to all people through spiritual renewal and rebirth. When Jesus ascended into heaven, his physical presence left the earth, but he promised to send the Holy Spirit so that his spiritual presence would still be among mankind (**Luke 24:49**). The Holy Spirit first became available to all believers at Pentecost (**Acts 20**). In the Old Testament days the Holy Spirit empowered individuals for specific purposes. Now all believers have the power of the Holy Spirit available to them.

We can't control the work of the Holy Spirit. He works in ways we can't predict or understand. The Holy Spirit is a gift from God.

Part of the Holy Spirit's job is to comfort us. Just like Jesus said when he returned to Heaven He promised he would send "The Comforter". "Holy" means without sin. The word of God tells us sin is going against God's laws. The Holy Spirit is a divine being (person, spirit) who has not sinned. I know a few things Holy Spirit does first hand because He has done plenty for me and others around me.

1) The Holy Spirit makes you aware of the sin in your life and teaches you what is right and wrong. He does this in many ways. For instance, causing your conscience to bother you when you do something you shouldn't and helping you to understand the right thing to do as you pray and read the Bible.

2) When you are going through a difficult time or situation. The Holy Spirit will give you strength, faith support and wisdom to help you through the tough time.

3) The Holy Spirit also gives you the boldness and courage to tell others about Jesus (which we call "witnessing"). Jesus expects you to share this wonderful experience (news) with others. Just

like you tell people about other things you are excited about like a wonderful vacation you took or a great movie you seen. Salvation is even more exciting, it's a beginning of a brand new life. You are a new person! You should want your family, friends and strangers to experience the same. As you try to explain it to others guess what the Holy Spirit will help you find the right words.

I have experienced the Holy Spirit numerous of times when I have started talking to someone about their issues or giving words to encourage someone or telling someone about Jesus and the words that come out of my mouth fit the person's situation and I didn't really know anything about their personal life. The Holy Spirit gives me the knowledge to help that person in their need. After the encounter is over and I think back and say where did that come from? I just open my mouth and start talking and everything just came out. I used to be afraid to talk to someone about something I am not very knowledgeable about or just didn't want to say anything wrong, but after this has happened to me several times the realization came to me it was the Holy Spirit that were giving me what to say.

The Holy Spirit is wonderful! Times when I had a family member pass or situation that was too intense for me to handle or when I thought I was not going to make it and it was too much! The Holy Spirit overtook me, comforted me, calmed me down and brought God's word to my remembrance about how Jesus loved me and God brought me through the last issue and He will bring me through this one too-amen, Thank you Lord!

The Holy Spirit is given to us by our Father out of obedience: **Acts 5:32** says, we are witnesses of these things and so is the Holy Spirit, who is given by God to those who obey him.

Here are some more examples of the Holy Spirit at work in the Bible. Please understand that you do not have to tarry (tarry means to wait on someone or something) for the Holy Spirit. The only time the disciples tarried or waited for the Holy Spirit was before He was poured out on the Day of Pentecost. They were tarrying in Jerusalem because that was the place where the Holy Spirit was initially going to be poured out.

The Holy Spirit gives us the boldness to speak what is right. **Acts 4:8** says then Peter, filled with the Holy Spirit said to them, Leaders and Elders . . . This lets you know he was speaking to people in high authority and of course he might have been nervous but with the Holy Spirit he has boldness to tell them what the Lord said on down through the chapter now at **Acts 4:13** says, the members of the council were amazed when they saw the boldness of Peter and John, for they could see that they were ordinary men who had no special training. They also recognized them as men who had been with Jesus. Regardless, of your background or education God can have people in high authority recognize the Jesus in you and knowledge beyond college-amen.

The Holy Spirit is also a comforter **Acts 8:31** says, The church then had peace throughout Judea, Galilee and Samaria and it grew in strength and numbers. The believers were walking in the fear of the Lord and in the comfort of the Holy Spirit.

The Holy Spirit can come while the word or message is being given **Acts 10:44** says, Even as Peter was saying these things, the Holy Spirit fell upon all who heard the message.

Well, I began telling them the Good News, but just as I was getting started, the Holy Spirit fell on them, just as he fell on us in the beginning. (**Acts 11:15**)

The Holy Spirit can tell you to go to a certain location. **Acts 11:12** says, The Holy Spirit told me to go with them and not to worry about their being Gentiles. This is wonderful, but I know for a while I didn't know the Holy Spirit was talking me when He would come across my mind telling me not to turn left, but turn right and go the longer route. I would still go left, because going right didn't make sense to me until when I got a few blocks down and found out traffic was locked due to an accident or there is a train on the track and now I'm stuck in the this stand still traffic because I did not listen to the Holy Spirit-which at the time I did not realize that was who it was. It has also been times when He has told me not to go to someone's house or to a party or gathering, because He knew it was going to be a fight or accident or something would occur that I did not need to be involved in. A lot of times lack of knowledge would say, "Something told me not to do that or go there or say that" but you did anyway and found out the complications were something you could have lived without.

The Holy Spirit will also remind you what you have been taught, especially when you are in situations that you need it for.

John 14:23-26: Jesus replied, "All those who love me will do what I say. My Father will love them and we will come to them and live with them. Anyone who doesn't love me will not do what I say. And remember, my words are not my own. This message is from the Father who sent me. I am telling you these things now while I am still with you. But when the Father sends the Counselor as my representative-and by the Counselor I mean the Holy Spirit-he will teach you everything and will remind you of everything I myself have told you.

Jesus had to leave for the Holy Spirit to come (the Counselor).

John 16:5-15 says, But now I am going away to the one who sent me, and none of you has asked me where I am going. Instead, you are very sad. But it is actually best for you that I go away, because if I don't, the Counselor won't come. If I do go away, he will come because I will send him to you. And when he comes, he will convince the world of its sin, and of God's righteousness is available because I go to the Father, and you will see me no more. Judgment will come because the prince of this world has already been judged. Oh, there is so much more I want to tell you, but you can't bear it now. When the Spirit of truth comes he will guide you into all truth. He will not be presenting his own ideas, he will be telling you what he has heard. He will tell you about the future. He will bring me glory by revealing to you whatever he receives from me. All that the Father has is mine; this is what I mean when I say that the Spirit will reveal to you whatever he receives from me.

The Holy Spirit helps us to pray. There are times where you will not know what to say, even a sound-moaning etc. God will still hear and know what you need through the Holy Spirit.

Romans 8:26-27 says, And the Holy Spirit helps us in our distress. For we don't even know what we should pray for, nor how we should pray, but the Holy Spirit prays for us with groanings that cannot be expressed in words. And the Father who knows all hearts knows what the Spirit is saying, for the Spirit pleads for us believers in harmony with God's own will.

Men in the bible were put in positions because they were filled with the Holy Spirit and also based on their reputation.

Acts 6:2-4 says, So the Twelve called a meeting of all the believers. "We apostles should spend our time preaching and teaching the word of God, not administering a food program," they said, "Now look around among yourselves, friends, and select seven men who are well respected and are full of the Holy Spirit and wisdom. We will put them in charge of this business. Then we can spend our time in prayer and preaching and teaching the word."

Now in my bible studies I came across this scripture which the Holy Spirit carried a person away-really.

Acts 8:35-40 says, So Philip began with this same scripture and then used many others to tell him the Good News about Jesus. As they road along, they came to some water and the eunuch said, "Look! There's some water! Why can't I be baptized?" He ordered the carriage to stop, and they went down into the water, and Philip baptized him. When they came up out of the water, the Spirit of the Lord caught Philip away. The eunuch never saw him again but went on his way rejoicing. Meanwhile, Philip found himself farther north at the city of Azotus! He preached the Good News there and in every city along the way until he came to Caesarea. Wow the Holy Spirit is so awesome! It seems to me there was some urgency to get Philip to this city to preach and teach the Good News.

God wants us to live by the Holy Spirit.

Gal 5:16-26 says, So I advise you to live according to your new life in the Holy Spirit. Then you won't be doing what your sinful nature craves. The old sinful nature loves to do evil, which is just opposite from what the Holy Spirit wants. And the Spirit gives us desires that are opposite from what the sinful nature desires. These two forces are constantly fighting each other, and your choices are never free from this conflict. But when you are directed by the Holy Spirit, you are no longer subject to the law.

When you follow the desires of your sinful nature, your lives will produce these evil results: sexual immorality, impure thoughts, eagerness for lustful pleasure, idolatry, participation in demonic activities, hostility, quarreling, jealousy, outbursts of anger, selfish ambition, divisions, the feeling that everyone is wrong except those in your own little group, envy, drunkenness, wild parties and other kinds of sin, Let me tell you again, as I have before, that anyone living that sort of life will not inherit the Kingdom of God.

But when the Holy Spirit controls our lives, he will produce this kind of fruit in us: love, joy, peace, patience, kindness, goodness, faithfulness, gentleness, and self-control. Here there is no conflict with the law.

Those who belong to Christ Jesus have nailed the passions and desires of their sinful nature to his cross and crucified them there. If we are living now by the Holy Spirit, let us follow the Holy Spirit's leading in every part of our lives. Let us not become conceited, or irritate one another, or be jealous of one another.

There is so much more about the Holy Spirit throughout the bible. Continue to study God's word and found out so much more about how the Holy Spirit can be utilized in your life.

CHAPTER 8

"CHURCH HOME"

I am going to let you know now there is no perfect church. I should know I have tried a few too many, one thing I learned is that when you look for a church home, please don't look for perfection but look for God's spirit and the word of God is being taught in excellence. You also need to know that everybody that goes to church are not going for the right reason.

Ask God to help you find a church. Some churches have different beliefs and they are broke down in what is called denominations. Your belief should match up with the church you want to attend. You also have to consider several things, like the size of the church. Some people like large churches, because they have more options for services, classes, programs and activities. In a large church you will probably make friends in Sunday school or small groups or while ministering. But some people like smaller churches because you get to know everybody one on one. Sometimes the drawback is there is not alot of classes or ministries to participate in or get a lot of people to join in. While small churches have the family atmosphere, but you should want your church to grow, because larger the small church gets just means more people have been added to the Kingdom of God. The bibles states they were added to the church daily.

I have attended churches where the current members had gotten attached to the Pastor and 1ˢᵗ lady and because they are used to the one on one attention, they tend to act like they don't want you to get a personal relationship with them for yourself. They still need to share their teaching, ministry and family love that was given to them. The new members deserve a chance to make their own relationships. Well for me in small churches I have to prove myself with the members what type of person I am, but the Pastor and 1ˢᵗ Lady always receive me in love. If it is the church you choose and you have a connection with the leaders, don't let the members turn you around. That is a trick of the enemy, stay, grow and be a blessing to the ministry.

A church is another term for the Body of Christ; a building where believers go to worship. A church home is a church you attend regularly, maybe you really like it and you join the church.

A church is a location where Christians gather to praise and worship God. Also, to receive the word of God and get understanding. The building is not the church the people make the church body.

1 Cor 12:12-31 says, the human body has many parts, but the many parts make up only one body. So it is with the body of Christ. Some of us are Jews, some are Gentiles, some are slaves, and some are free. But we have all been baptized into Christ's body by one Spirit and we have all received the same Spirit.

Yes, the body has many different parts, not just one part, if the foot says, "I am not a part of the body because I am not a hand" that does not make it any less a part of the body. And if the ear says, "I am not a part of the body because I am only an ear and not an eye," would that make it any less a part of the body? Suppose the whole body were an eye-then how would you hear? Or if your whole body were just one big ear, how could you smell anything?

But God made our bodies with many parts, and he has put each part just where he wants it, what a strange thing a body would be if it had only one part! Yes, there are many parts, but only one body. The eye can never say to the hand, "I don't need you." The head can't say to the feet, "I don't need you."

In fact, some of the parts that seem weakest and least important are really the most necessary. And the parts we regard as less honorable are those we clothe with the greatest care. So we carefully protect from the eyes of others those parts that should not be seen, while other parts do not require this special care. So God has put the body together in such a way that extra honor and care are given to those parts that have less dignity. This makes for harmony among the members care for each other equally. If one part suffers, all the parts suffer with it, and if one part is honored, all the parts are glad.

Now all of you together are Christ's body, and each one of you is separate and necessary part of it. Here is a list of some of the members that God has placed in the body of Christ:

First are apostles, second are prophets, third are teachers, then those who do miracles, those who have the gift of healing, those who can help others, those who can get others to work together, those who speak in unknown languages.

Is everyone an apostle? Of course not is everyone a prophet? No. Are all teachers? Does everyone have the power to do miracles? Does everyone have the gift of healing? Of course not. Does God give all of us the ability to speak unknown languages? Can everyone interpret unknown languages? No! And in any event, you should desire the most helpful gift.

You need to know that everybody can't do the same thing and God has called you and put a gift in you that will be needed at the church you attend. Even if you attend a church that does not have a ministry or they are not doing what God has given you to do, does not mean you can't start something new. Make sure that you do it in order and contact the correct person and present what you do and how you can go about presenting it.

I am not being mean or saying this to upset anyone, but we live in the real world and we have not gone to Heaven yet and we live where people do bad things even in church. Please keep up with your children and make sure they are safe. Do not let your small children go to the restroom alone or run around the church alone. Like I said before, everyone in church is not "saved", or "delivered" or there for the right reason, so stay ALERT! If you have noticed the churches have been in the news for several different reasons within the last five years. So, use wisdom in all you do not only with your children but yourself-amen.

I know sometimes when you visit a church, you see people looking mean, not speaking or smiling, but God says it should be different. The bible says we should be glad.

Psalms 122:1 says, I was glad when they said to me "Let us go to the house of the Lord."

We should treat everyone with love, especially our Christian family.

Gal 6:10 says, Whenever we have the opportunity, we should do good to everyone, especially to our Christian brothers and sisters.

The church is where you should get instruction from God's word. You should also read God's Word for yourself on a daily basis. But, our gathering together is important. The primary reason for going to church is to worship God. You were created to worship Him. Jesus died so you could be saved from sin. He is your provider and protector. He cares about our life. Attending church is a simple way to show love, appreciation and honor to God.

We have to be patient with each other. We are all not on the same level of spirituality, for example: God has delivered you from an "issue" and a Christian brother or sister is around you and they have the same issue you did, but you just can't take it. It's is too much for you, they should be delivered, it's not that serious. But, remember how long it took you and how much patience God had with you. You can't put a timeframe on God working in someone's life. He may use you to be a light to help another person to let them see God can deliver them from their issue. And when that issue is resolved something new will be brought to your mind. For instance you were delivered from cursing and you feeling good about it and then it comes to your mind that you tell white lies, but we all know a lie is a lie and He starts working on you telling the truth all the time and learning how to tell the truth tactfully, to make sure you say it not to hurt a person's feeling which you were trying to avoid by telling those lies in the beginning. Now you are delivered from that and now it is brought to your mind you are not spending enough time with your spouse and children so you start working on that. God will work on us until He returns.

We have to remember because sometimes we forget we had some of those same issues the person around you has and God worked with you and He still is.

Eph 2:1-10 says, once you were dead, doomed forever because of your many sins. You used to live just like the rest of the world, full of sin, obeying satan, the mighty prince of the power of the air. He is the spirit at work in the hearts of those who refuse to obey God. All of us used to live that way, following the passions and desires of our evil nature. We were born with evil, and we were under God's anger just like everyone else.

But God is so rich in mercy, and he loved us so very much, that even while we were dead because of our sins, he gave us life when he raised Christ from the dead. It is only by God's special favor that you have been saved! For he raised us from the dead along with Christ. And so God can always point to us as examples of the incredible wealth of his favor and kindness towards us, as shown in all he has done for us through Christ Jesus. God saved you by his special favor when you believed. And you can't take credit for this; it is a gift from God.

Salvation is not a reward for the good things we have done, so none of us can boast about it. For we are God's masterpiece. He has created us anew in Christ Jesus, so that we can do the good things he planned for us long ago.

Like I said be patient with each other in love.

Eph 4:1-6 says, Therefore I, a prisoner for serving the Lord, beg you to lead a life worthy of your calling, for you have been called by God. Be humble and gentle. Be patient with each other, making allowances for each other's faults because of your love. Always keep yourselves united in the Holy Spirit, and bind yourselves together with peace. We are all one body, we have the same Spirit, and we have all been called to the same glorious future. There is only one Lord, one faith, one baptism, and there is only one God and Father, who is over us all and and living through us all.

When you are searching for a church make sure it accommodates you and your family. You want your whole family to be ministered to. You also want to make sure you can understand what is being taught. You really want to be under a Pastor that teaches the word of God and rightly divides the word-meaning so you can understand and apply it to your life.

I have found some Pastors that preach instead of teach and get on the "run way doc"-meaning they may say one scripture and the rest of the sermon they are hooping, hollering and screaming. I also heard them hoop and then play on the organ "Mary had a little lamb"-wow, no teaching or understanding. God wants His word to be taught clearly. Jesus took his time to tell parables (short stories) to explain the word on the listener's level.

God wants us to know his word and apply it to our lives and not be a "barren" fig tree. We want to bare fruit, there should be evidence of who we are.

Luke 13:6-9 says, Then Jesus used this illustration: "a man planted a fig tree in his garden and came again and again to see if there was any fruit on it, but he was always disappointed. Finally, he said to the gardener, "I've waited three years, and there hasn't been a single fig. Cut it down. It's taking up space we can use for something else. The gardener answered, "Give it one more chance, leave it another year, and I'll give it special attention and plenty of fertilizer. If we get figs next year, fine, if not, you can cut it down.

When you become a member of a church, you have become a part of the Kingdom of God. **Matt 6:33** says, But seek ye the Kingdom of God and His righteousness.

Being a Christian as well as a member of a church takes commitment-which means to do, to devote or pledge (oneself) to the doing of something. For a lot of people it is hard to commit and that is why there is a lot of bench warmers or bench members which means they come to church to get the word, but will not get involved in anything else. They will not participate in any ministry or serving of any kind. But God's word says we are all needed for God's Kingdom work.

We should attend church to help us or show us how to be committed to living your life for the Kingdom of God and following the teachings of Jesus Christ. I find when I attend church and give my praise and worship to God he lifts my burdens and issues of life.

Matt 11:28 says, Then Jesus said, "Come to me all of you who are weary and carry heavy burdens, and I will give you rest. Take my yoke upon you. Let me teach you, because I am humble and gentle and you will find rest for your souls. For my yoke fits perfectly and the burdens I give you will be light."

You also attend church to learn and grow in God's word.

2Pet 3:18 says, but grow in grace and knowledge of our Lord and Savior Jesus Christ. To him be the glory both now and forever amen! Going to church helps you develop your relationship with Jesus and more about being a Christian. When you attend church it gives you an opportunity to learn more about God during church services, Sunday school classes, special groups and bible studies.

Another reason we attend church is to build relationships with other Christians and come to encourage one another. **Heb 3:13** says, but encourage one another daily as long as it is called today, so that none of you may be hardened by sin deceitfulness. When you accepted Christ-our Father God adopted us and we became part of His family. We need a family who can encourage us through difficult times and cheer for our achievements.

Acts 2:42 says, They joined with other believers and devoted themselves to the apostles teaching and fellowship, sharing in the Lord's supper and prayer. Wow, this says we should spend time together first listening to the teaching, the word of God coming forth, so we can get the same word. We are learning together as a family.

Next, He wants us to fellowship, so when the Pastor says in service to get up and go shake someone's hand or give them a hug-don't get upset and start mouthing off. This is what God wants His children to do. He wants us to get to know one another, so when a fellowship is set up, for instance: a picnic, bowling, movie night etc. try to make some of the fellowships this a time to get to know one another aside from church. You can see the people that are usually so serious at church, be so playful and funny in another atmosphere and you would never know that if you didn't fellowship. So, if a new person starts attending your church and they say, "oh Ms. Smith looks so mean all the time" and you can be able to say, "you just have to get to know her, she is so funny and makes the best sweet potato pies." See what I mean, but you have to get to know one another to have that information.

The next thing He wanted for us to do in this scripture was for us to share in the Lord's Supper. Which to me should be a family thing, just like dinner time-back in the old days everyone sat down to dinner together and did not start eating until everyone was there. When I used to visit my grandmother, we could not eat until granddaddy got home or she called him and he was still working or was not close to home and told her to let the kids go ahead and eat, because he was running late. But their household understood eating together as a family. God wants His kids to eat together and remember His son together.

Last but not least, based on this scripture He wants us to pray together! Praise God! He wants us to be on one accord in communicating with Him. He is our Father and He took the time to let us know he wants us to play together, treat each other right, spend time together, eat together and talk to him together. Amen!

When we attend church we are being a good example to others. Jesus attended church (the bible sometimes says "synagogue) and on the Sabbath day He went into the synagogue.

Luke4:16 says, He went to Nazareth, where he had been brought up and on the Sabbath day he went into the synagogue as his custom. And he stood up and read.

God does not want us to forsake our meeting together as Christians. He wants us as his children to spend time together.

I have heard so many times from Christians, "I will just stay at home and watch church on television." Unless you are physically unable to attend church, God wants us to meet together (assemble together).

Hebrews 10:25 says, Let us not give up meeting together as some are in the habit of doing, but let us encourage one another and all the more as you see the day approaching.

To neglect Christian meetings is to give up the encouragement and help of other Christians. We gather together to share our faith and to strengthen one another in the Lord. As we gather together to share our faith and to strengthen one another in the Lord. As we get closer to the "Day" when Christ will return, we will face many spiritual struggles and even times of persecution. The anti-Christian forces will grow in strength. Difficulties should never be excuses for missing church services. Rather, when difficulties arise, we should make an even greater effort to be faithful in attendance. There is strength in numbers-go to church and be with your fellow Christians and defeat the enemy. That is what he wants you to do is feel defeated. He wants you to stay home and think nobody cares what I am going through, but that is not true. Go to church and let them know what is going on with you and you will see what God and your Christian family can do. Have you heard the old saying, "a closed mouth won't get feed" amen!

Church attendance is not only important for adults, but also for our children. In the past, I have asked a fellow Christian, where is your son or daughter and they would tell me they left them at home, because they weren't ready or they were tired or something. I'm sorry in my household everybody goes to church. If it is not the church I attend it will need to be somebody's church. If they are still of child age they need to go where you attend, definitely if they have the classes for them. But, it wasn't until my son was an adult where he was given the ability or permission to attend another church other than the one I attend. I believe that a family should receive the same word so there will be no misunderstandings.

I have seen in the past married couples going to separate churches and I am not knocking that, but I want my husband to receive the same word I do, so he will know when he is wrong and I won't have to try to explain it to him from scratch. (I'm kidding) I would rather for him to be at church in person especially when they are teaching the men how to love their wives amen! Which is not often-another joke-I am getting back on the subject.

Teaching our children is very important. By teaching them how God wants us to live will better equip them to deal with problems. We want to make sure they know God loves them and will always see them through. When we equip our children guess what, they go out and make disciples like them, their age. A lot of times a child will listen to another child before they listen to adult (go figure, but we did the same thing as a kid-one time or another). So, why not make sure good things are in them, so good things can come out, especially about how God loves them and wants all his children to go to Heaven-amen.

Remember, when searching for a church pray about it. It is very important that they are friendly. Also, review all programs, classes offered. Make sure the leadership is approachable. Can the church meet your needs? Are you able to serve in ministry? Does the church let you use your gifts & talents?

For example: if you have children, does the church have classes or programs for your kids and do they enjoy it and they are learning the word of God?

God bless you in finding a wonderful church to fit you and your family needs!

There's lots of reasons to attend church, but one of the main purposes is to praise and worship our Lord!

The bible gives us an example of "Orderly Worship", in **1Cor 14:25-33** says, Well, my brothers and sisters, let's summarize what I am saying. When you meet, one will sing, another will teach, another will tell some special revelation God has given, one will speak in unknown language, while another will interpret what is said. But everything that is done must be useful to all and build them up in the Lord. No more than two or three should speak in an unknown language. They must speak one at a time, and someone must be ready to interpret what they are saying. But if no one is present who can interpret, they must be silent in your church meeting and speak in tongues to God privately.

Let two or three prophesy, and let the others evaluate what is said. But if someone is prophesying and another person receives a revelation from the

Lord, the one who is speaking must stop. In this way, all who prophesy will have a turn to speak, one after the other, so that everyone will learn and be encouraged. Remember that people who prophesy are in control of their spirit and can wait their turn. For God is not a God of disorder but of peace, as in all the other churches.

1Cor 14:39-40 says, So dear brothers and sisters, be eager to prophesy and don't forbid speaking in tongues. But be sure that everything is done properly and in order.

Remember that God wants us to praise and worship! He wants us to teach our babies and children to praise and worship him! He also wants us to be decent and in order! Love your God and show him on a daily basis through your praise and worship! Amen

CHAPTER 9

"PRAYER"

Prayer is very simple, communication with God and Jesus. Communication contains talking and listening. Sometimes people consider prayer most of all requesting the desires that one needs like healing or covering someone from harm or helping someone to direct their path from evil to good.

When I was young I remember my mom having us kneel on the side of the bed for prayer. She told us to repeat after her, she said:

Now I lay me down to sleep, if I should die before I wake-I pray the Lord my soul to take. Amen

Throughout my Christian life I have heard people say they had prayer closets (literally a closet). A certain place they pray. Praying when they woke, praying before they went to sleep, praying over their food, praying over their children, praying over their family members, prayer request from others etc. it can go on and on.

Now that you are a new Christian it is important for you get to know God on a personal basis. One way is to think of God as your new friend you just met. You need to spend time each day talking to Him and letting Him talk to you. Some people call this having their quiet time or their devotion, but it doesn't matter what you call it as long as you do it!

You might be thinking, "How do you talk to somebody you can't see? Isn't that kind of strange? And what's this whole business about God talking to me? I mean, isn't He supposed to be busy running the universe or something?" Well, the good news is that even though He is running the universe, He still wants to communicate with you, and He has provided you with a couple of really great tools that will help you do that: the Bible and prayer.

There isn't one specific way that God says you have to pray, but there are some guidelines you may want to use.

As you begin to pray, make sure you don't have sin in your life that you haven't confessed. The Bible says that if we cherish (or hold on to) sin in our hearts, God won't listen.

Psalms 66:18 says, If I had not confessed the sin in my heart, my Lord would not have listened.

So it's important to ask God to show you how you've sinned and ask Him to forgive you before you go any further in your prayer. Simply say something like, "God, if there is anything I thought or said that was wrong?" You may want to think over the past day or so and think if God points out something to you. If He does, tell Him you see where you were wrong, and ask Him to forgive you. The Bible says, "If you confess your sins, He is faithful and just and will forgive us our sins" (**1John 1:9**). So you can be sure that once you have admitted your sins and asked for forgiveness, God has forgiven you.

Since you are God's child, He wants to give you all you need just like human parents want to provide for their children. You can ask God for anything, and He won't be surprised. The Bible says, "Ask and it will be given to you" (**Luke 11:9** says, And so I tell you, keep on asking, and you will be given what you ask for. Keep on looking, and you will find. Keep on knocking and the door will be opened. For everyone who seeks, finds. And the door is opened.) and "I tell you the truth, my Father will give you whatever you ask in my name (**John 16:23**). Does this mean that you get everything you ask for? Obviously not, or everyone in the world would become a Christian just so they could have all the money, power, or fame they wanted. A good parent doesn't give his child everything they want, either. He knows that some things you ask for aren't the best things for you, and some things are actually harmful. He also knows the future, so sometimes when He says "no" to your request, it's because He has something even better waiting for you.

The more you pray, the better you'll understand God and how He works in the world. You will find that as you grow as a Christian, your prayers will start sounding different. You'll start asking more for things you know God wants you to have, and less for things you don't need. Praise and confession will come more easily, too, as you grow to know and love Him more.

Prayer and Bible reading can be hard work, but they're worth it. Growing as a Christian takes time, you must start slowly and gradually increase the time and effort you put into your praying and Bible reading each day. As you do, you will be rewarded to find that you are beginning to speak, act, and think more like God wants you to every day.

2Cor 5:9 says, "So we make it our goal to please Him."

Here are some scriptures about prayer:

Prayer should be just for our Lord God. **Psalms 5:1-3** says, O Lord, hear me as I pray; pay attention to my groaning. Listen to my cry for help, my King and my God, for I will never pray to anyone but you. Listen to my voice in the morning, Lord. Every morning I bring my requests to you and wait expectantly.

Jesus taught his disciples to pray. **Matt 6:7-15** says, When you pray, don't babble on and on as people of other religions do. They think their prayers are answered only by repeating their words again and again. Don't be like them, because your Father knows exactly what you need even before you ask him! Pray like this: Our Father in Heaven, may your name be honored. May your kingdom come soon. May your will be done here on earth, just as it is in Heaven. Give us our food for today, and forgive us our sins, just as we have forgiven those who have sinned against us. And don't let us yield to temptation, but deliver us from the evil one.

If you forgive those who sin against you, your heavenly Father will forgive you. But if you refuse to forgive others, your Father will not forgive your sins. But If you refuse to forgive others, your Father will not forgive your sins.

Pray in Jesus name. **John 16:23-24** says, At that time you won't need to ask me for anything. The truth is, you can go directly to the Father and ask Him, and he will grant your request because you use my name. You haven't done this before. Ask using my name, and you will receive and you will have abundant joy.

CHAPTER 10

"PRAISE & WORSHIP"

Wow! This is one of my favorites, Praise and worship! I love to give God the Praise and Worship He deserves, that is due him. He deserves that and more for what He has done. If He doesn't do another thing He has done so much for me.

I just can't tell it all from God saving me as a child, blacking in and out while riding in an ambulance because I can't breathe due to asthma attacks and when I became an adult and found out that people die from that issue daily, but God saw fit to save my life and breathe breath back into me for such a time as this. There are so many times God has saved my life, once I was driving home and I fell asleep. The jerk of the car woke me which was a standard. I was at a traffic light not too far from my house. The last thing I remember before falling asleep was going a back road and had to go over a train track and was not woke for any of that. Tell me God ain't good!

I remember waking up to a smoke filled apartment being able to get to the kitchen and seeing fire shooting from the stove, but God gave the grace for me to put it out and open the windows and doors and get my family out safe without injury to apartment or us. To walk away from a wreck where I was the passenger in a neon (which is a very small car) to be hit so hard by a large dump truck and be dragged a football field of the freeway, to see myself inside the car looking from above. I could see the driver laying over on me because she didn't wear her seatbelt. When God brought me back to myself and then I started feeling something warm on my legs-it was her blood not mine. My knees were in pain, the back of the car was smashed up on us and the baby car seat was up through the roof. The windshield was broke all over us-glass was in my head and face. I could hear them cutting us out the car and the same day I was back home when just some bumps and bruises and the driver had extensive injuries which included broken ribs and had to have her spleen removed etc.

Tell me to praise God! You don't have to because I am going to praise Him anyhow. I am sure you can think about something that God has done for you! I can't count how many times he has saved me from death, danger and my mind being lost. Yes, losing my mind, don't think that is a game. There are plenty of people in those places, where they are walking around talking to themselves because they have lost their mind. I thank God he has kept my mind. Even when I thought it was slipping away He came and rescued me. Boy, you guys are going to make me shout up in here! Lord have mercy! Thank you Lord for all you have done for me! Praise God!

Let me finish telling you about Praise and worship—I got a little excited! I just love God and His Son and I am not ashamed to show it or tell it! Let's start with some definitions:

Praise means to applaud, compliment, glorify, commend, acclaim, flatter, admire & celebrate!

Worship means to honor, revere, adore, reverence, glorify and respect!

To get more physical "Praise and Worship" consists of dancing, running, raising your hands, jumping, clapping, bowing, kneeling, laying face down or it could even be playing an instrument, singing, signing, miming, it could be a number of things that you can do to praise and worship God.

Actually, Praise and worship is a personal relationship you have with God. It's how you want to reverence Him! I might not worship the same way my neighbor standing beside me at church does. I maybe raising my hands and she may be jumping and shouting. No one is wrong, it is a individual expression to our Lord.

Praise is faster movement or pace, because the songs are moderate to fast. Worship is a slow movement or pace, because the songs are slower-almost like a love song. Praise and worship is not just to be done at church, but also—at home, or in your car. But, remember in your car keep your hands on the wheel and your eyes open-amen!

You can praise and worship God anytime or anywhere. God created you to praise and worship Him! Praise and worship is just expressing love to God, because of who He is!

Matt 22:37-Jesus replied, "Love the Lord your God with all your heart and with all your soul and with all your mind."

The word says we should worship God because He is Holy.

Psalms 29:2 says, Give honor to the Lord, for the glory of His name. Worship the Lord in the splendor of his holiness.

We should praise God through whatever we are going through.

Psalms 30:11-12 says, You have turned my mourning into joyful dancing. You have taken away my clothes of mourning and clothed me with joy, that I might sing praises to you and not be silent. O Lord my God, I will give you thanks forever!

We are not to worship any other God, person or thing.

Luke 4:8 says, Jesus answered, "It is written. Worship the Lord your God and serve Him only."

When my son tells me he loves me and that I am the best mom he ever had (smile) and that he thanks me for cooking his favorite meals and being there for him. He says he loves me this much-lol-you can't see it, but I can and it is his way of expressing the love he has for me. I love to hear those things! God feels the same way. When His children praise and worship Him, I believe He loves to hear the appreciation. Love God the way our children love us. They love us for who we are, not what we do for them! (Now there are special exclusions of different parent and child relationship, but it should be genuine).

Praise and worship is basically showing respect, love and admiration to God. When you worship God you are honoring Him. You are acknowledging that He is the one true God and your focus is on Him.

Every person worships God in his own way, it should be a personal expression that comes from your heart!

Don't worry if it is difficult for you to worship God now. As your relationship with God grows, you will get over your fears. Remember the focus of worship is God!

Standing is part of honoring God out respect, just like when the president walks into the room. Everyone stands out of respect to his position. God deserves the same.

Neh 9:5 says, "Stand up and praise the Lord your God, who is from everlasting to everlasting."

Kneeling is a sign of respect, honor and humility.

Psalms 95:6 says, "Come let us bow down in worship, let us kneel before the Lord our maker, for he is our God." You're acknowledging God's power and strength. You respect who He is and you recognize He is worthy of praise!

Psalms 134:2 says, Lift your hands in holiness, and bless the Lord.

We should sing, you may be thinking I can't sing, but God doesn't say—only sing to me if you can sing. Just open your mouth and give him the praise!

Psalms 81:1-2 says, Sing praises to God, our strength. Sing! Beat the tambourine. Play the sweet lyre and the harp.

We should give thanks through singing.

Col 3:16 says, Let the words of Christ, in all their richness, live in your hearts and make you wise. Use his words to teach and counsel each other. Sing psalms and hymns and spiritual songs to God with thankful hearts.

Eph 5:19-20 says, Then you will sing psalms and hymns and spiritual songs among yourselves, making music to the Lord in your hearts. And you will always give thanks for everything to God the Father in the name of our Lord Jesus Christ.

We should praise Him all the time.

Psalms 34:1 says, I will praise the Lord at all times. I will constantly speak his praises.

We should teach our babies to praise God. I have actually been in the sanctuary when babies were in church from birth and seeing 1 year olds raise their hands to praise the Lord! Also, seeing them clapping and even trying to sing the songs they hear us singing! It makes my heart jump for joy!

Psalms 8:2 says, You have taught children and nursing infants to give you praise. They silence your enemies who were seeking revenge.

Kids learn from what is put in front of them and what they are taught. So, make sure everything you put in front of them is positive.

Praise and worship is usually accompanied with music. Make sure you find praise and worship stations on your radio. You can go on the web and find music you will enjoy. You can also go to a Christian bookstore and go to the music section and you can listen to some soundtracks or cds to find music you like and will enjoy during your praise and worship time at home or in your car.

Music calms you down and makes you think, so make sure you choose meaningful music. You will know it when you hear it, because you will feel it inside. Sometimes when I am in my car and I put in a Yolanda Adams cd in and some of her songs just make tears come to my eyes, because she makes me think of how much God loves me. Marvin Sapp, Jeremy Camp, Kurt Carr, Donnie McClurkin, Cece Winans, Smokie Norful, James Fortune & Fiya and Shekinah Glory Ministries are a few more artists that bring tears to my eyes and give me that closeness with God. You will find your own favorites and know what to listen to when you have a mood you need music for. I am a music person, so I love all kind of music and have certain songs for certain moods!

Enjoy Praising and Worshiping God alone, with family and at church! Amen

CHAPTER 11

"FASTING?"

Fasting means to abstain from food mostly known for a religious discipline. I have found throughout the years, you can fast from more than just food. I have attended a church where we were challenged to the "Daniel fast", which consist of eating only fruit and vegetables for forty days. Which is referred to a book in the Bible about Daniel and some of his men ate only vegetables and fruit and were stronger and healthier because of it. (**Daniel 1:8-20**)

Jesus taught about fasting: **Matt 6:16-18** says, when you fast, do not look somber as the hypocrites do, for they disfigure their face to show men they are fasting. I will tell you the truth, they have received their reward in full. But when you fast, put oil on your head and wash your face, so that it will not be obvious to men that you are fasting, but only to your Father, who is unseen; and your Father who sees what is done in secret, will reward you.

Jesus was not condemning fasting, but hypocrisy—fasting in order to gain public approval. It was mandatory for the Jewish people once a year on the Day of Atonement. But Jesus was against making it a show to get attention.

Lev 23:32 says, "This will be a Sabbath day of total rest for you and on that day you must humble yourselves. This time of rest and fasting will begin the evening before the Day of Atonement and extend until evening of the next day."

The Pharisees voluntarily fasted twice a week to impress the people with their "holiness." Jesus commended acts of self-sacrifice done quietly and sincerely. He wanted people to adopt spiritual disciplines for the right reasons, not from a selfish desire for praise.

Fasting-going without food in order to spend time in prayer-is noble and difficult. It gives us time to pray, teaches self—discipline and reminds us we can live with a lot less. Also, helps us to appreciate God's gifts.

Fasting also sets you apart to do the work of the Lord.

Acts 13:2 says, While they were worshiping the Lord and fasting, the Holy Spirit said, "set apart for me Barnabas and Saul for the work to which I have called them." So after they had fasted and prayed, they placed their hands on them and sent them off.

The church set apart Barnabas and Saul for the work God had for them. To set apart means to dedicate for a special purpose.

Some people may complain or voice their opinion or just give excuses about not doing a fast, but don't be distracted. The times I've done a fast changed came into my life, not only that but doors were opened-where the enemy tried to distract me with illness, family issues, friends mistreating me and as well and new enemies rising up.

Just as I got to this part of the book the church I attend was beginning a forty day fast. What's funny is it was right before Thanksgiving and was going through Christmas-our Bishop let's the Lord lead him like that. It was not just for food, but whatever God laid on us to fast from. It could have been television, computers, drinks, relationships, the list could go on. Well, while the fast was going I was working on this book and I get a call my brother was stabbed in his lung near his heart and he was close to death, so me, mom and son rush to the hospital and I am texting my church family to start praying for him. Praise God he made it through that surgery and hospital stay and he went home with my mom. In the meantime I was getting ill-like a virus. I called my doctor and he was out of town and would not be back until the next week and the day of my appointment it snowed and if you know me I don't even drive in rain, if I can help it. Well, I woke up and said I guess I better go, because I have something else to talk to the doctor about. I had a growth on my head and I wanted him to check it out and he referred me to another doctor the same week, which was on a Thursday. Well, I go to the specialist and the moment he sees the growth, he says I am scheduling you for surgery on Monday-wow, ok. They wanted to make sure it was not cancerous. I bind that in the name of Jesus-amen.

Well, my son was with me and he is encouraging me that it is going to be alright. I drop him off and go to work and I get a call from my mom, that my brother was in pain and couldn't breathe and she had to send him in an ambulance to the hospital. I told her to call me back and let me know what is going on. I sent out texts for my church family to start praying. She calls me back within 30 minutes and says, "He is going into emergency surgery." Well, remember when he got stabbed the first time in his lung near his heart. The knife did hit his heart the first time and it had been bleeding from the initial hospital stay and the surgeon told us later on that night after he had been in surgery for hours—that his heart was bleeding and creating blood clots around his heart and his lungs and he could have died at any time-any moment. The surgeon said he did all he could do and the rest was left up to God. (wow-he was a believer) My brother came out the surgery fine and recovering.

I had evaluation at my job that I have been at for almost 6 years and do the best to my ability every day. I help my co-workers and go above and beyond each day I am there, but my evaluation showed the opposite. I know it was the enemy trying to distract me and upset me. Instantly, I was upset-but in a few minutes I had to think clearly and recognized what it really was.

Now, it's Monday and time for my surgery-the previous Sunday I asked my sisters in Christ to pray for me, so at that moment they took their time to lay hands on me and pray. The hospital stay was scheduled to be from 12n-3p, but actually ended up being to 7p. I was so very sick after the surgery. When I got home I was throwing up all night. My mom and son stayed with me to help me through the night. My son had been without a job for over a year and he just got a job and they fired him, because he was at the hospital with me.

My mom is in her 60's having medical issues of her own and trying to take care of my brother and being there for me. All I told the church was I don't need anything but your prayers. My Bishop's wife has been wonderful and consistently texting and checking on me. She is always asking me if I need anything to let her know. I just love her spirit!

What I am showing you is that "fasting" brings open doors and my only response is "prayer" and that I have to stay encouraged in the Lord! I know what He has done for me for the past 41 years, so I can't doubt now, because my faith has been built over years. In the past I would be upset and let myself get sicker and sicker by being upset and speaking negatively. But God has been so good to me regardless of what is in the natural.

In the past I was told that the more things come out that means God has a blessing for you. The next day after my surgery-I received a call that a lady that saw my play "Lord, Why me?" that I wrote, wanted me to bring it to her church in a nearby town. God has use for me and you.

Job in the Bible kept his faith through situations that were way more difficult than mine and God blessed him for his endurance and keeping his faith through his trials.

There are many fasts or should I say many ways to fast: all water fast; no food fast; fruit and vegetable only fast; juice only fast or fast from "habits."

A fast is a commitment of putting God first. Giving yourself to prayer and setting your mind on what you need to do for God's Kingdom.

While I was on this fast, I saw things more clearly-like who was for me and who was not. I instantly receive alertness of what I was doing or saying wrong. More ideas and thoughts of what I wanted to do for God's Kingdom came to me.

With fasting comes temptation. An example would be the "The temptation of Jesus". He was on an absolute fast-no food or water.

Matt 4:1-11 says, Then Jesus was led out into the wilderness by the Holy Spirit to be tempted there by the devil. For forty days and forty nights he ate nothing and became very hungry. Then the devil came and said to him, "If you are the Son of God", change these stones into loaves of bread." But, Jesus told him, "No! The Scriptures say, "People need more than bread for their life; they must feed on every word of God." Then the devil took him to Jerusalem, to the highest point of the Temple and said, "If you are the Son of God, jump off! For the Scriptures say, "He orders his angels to protect you. And they will hold you with their hands to keep you from striking your foot on a stone." Jesus responded, "The Scriptures also say, "Do not test the Lord your God." Next the devil took him to the peak of the very high mountain and showed him the nations of the world and all their glory, I will give it all to you, he said, "if you will only kneel down and worship me.' Get out of here satan," Jesus told him, "For the Scriptures say, You must worship the Lord your God; serve only him." Then the devil went away, and the angels came and cared for Jesus.

Throughout Jesus being tempted his put the Word of God on the devil and then told him to flee. You have to know the word to use it. He also kept the faith in what he already knew. Then satan tried to distract him and turn the word around to mean something different. But Jesus recognized the satan was trying to mislead him. Jesus had the victory over satan, because he kept the Word of God in his heart and he used it when trouble came.

There is also fasting in marriage, I know you are wondering what is she talking about. You see God thought of everything.

1Cor 7:5-6 says, So do not deprive each other of sexual relations. The only exception to this rule would be the agreement of both husband and wife to refrain from sexual intimacy for a limited time, so they can give themselves more completely to prayer. Afterward they should come together again, so that satan won't be able to tempt them because of their lack of self-control.

As you see throughout the scriptures there were temptations, but staying with the word of God and not being swayed brings blesses at the end. God sent the angels to take care of Jesus.

Every fast is not the same, so don't compare your fast to someone else's. What you go through and the results are between you and God. You should learn something throughout the time of your fast. You should move to another level, it may not be what you think you should get from it, but it is God's will.

Also, remember to fast and pray. Prayer and the word of God will give you continued strength throughout your fast.

Jesus is able to help us through any temptation.

Heb 2:18 says, Since he himself has gone through suffering and temptation. He is able to help us when we are being tempted.

When you fast, don't give up!

2Cor 4:8-9 says, We are pressed on every side by troubles, but we are not crushed and broken. We are perplexed, but we don't give up and quit. We are hunted down, but God never abandons us. We get knocked down, but we get up again and keep going.

God bless you!

CHAPTER 12

"PASTORS AND LEADERS"

This a sensitive subject to me because God gave us Pastors and leaders in his church to love us and guide us in the right direction, but that doesn't happen all the time. It is very unfortunate that is why you need to know what to look for. You shouldn't be misused or abused by any leader. Some have used their position in error. I have attended churches where the leaders were a God sent and some I thought came from the opposite direction of Heaven. But remember there is no perfect leader, but they should strive to be what God describes in the Bible. So, let's go to the word of God.

Leaders are gifts from God.

Eph 4:11 says, He is the one who gave these gifts to the church; the apostles, the prophets, the evangelists and the pastors and teachers.

They are to equip us to do Kingdom work.

Eph 4:12-13 says, Their responsibility is to equip God's people to do his work and build up the church, the body of Christ, until we come to such unity in our faith and knowledge of God's son that we will be mature and full grown in the Lord, measuring up to the full statue of Christ.

They should be after God's own heart.

Jere 3:15 says, And I will give you leaders after my own heart, who will guide you with knowledge and understanding.

God has criteria for his leaders.

Titus 1:6-9 says, An elder must be well thought of for his good life. He must be faithful to his wife and his children must be believers who are not wild or rebellious. An elder must live a blameless life because he is God's minister. He must not be a heavy drinker, violent or greedy for money. He must enjoy having guests in his home and must love all that is good. He must live wisely and be fair. He must live a devout and disciplined life. He must have a strong and steadfast belief in the trustworthy message he was taught; then he will be able to encourage others with right teaching and show those who oppose it where they are wrong.

They should be able to deal with difficult people.

2Tim 2:23-26 says, Again I say, don't get involved in foolish, ignorant arguments that only start fights. The Lord's servants must not quarrel but must be able to teach effectively and be patient with difficult people. They should gently teach those who oppose the truth, perhaps God will change those people's hearts, and they will believe the truth. Then they will come to their senses and escape from the devils trap. For they have been held captive by him to do whatever he wants.

They should show they are true ministers of God.

2Cor 6:3-4 says, We try to live in such a way that no one will be hindered from finding the Lord by the way we act, so no one can find fault with our ministry. In everything we do we try to show that we are true ministers of God. We patiently endure troubles and hardships and calamities of every kind.

Sometimes preachers teach on general subjects, but don't get too deep in our business and they should tell us what we need to know, which is the truth to help us change ourselves and guess what we should honor them for it.

1Thess 5:12-13 says, Dear brothers and sisters, honor those who are your leaders in the Lord's work. They work hard among you and warn you against all that is wrong. Think highly of them and give then your wholehearted love because of their work. And remember to live peaceably with each other.

The message that is taught to us should be plain in order for us to understand. How can we use the message in our lives if we don't understand it?

1Cor 2:4-5 says, And my message and my preaching were very plain. I did not use wise and persuasive speeches, but the Holy Spirit was powerful among you. I did this so that you might trust the power of God rather than human wisdom.

The Pastor should follow through on what is right. If he is aware of open sin in the church, it should be addressed based on God's word. (Please read **1 Cor 5:1-13**)

God has chosen the preachers to teach us the truth. **1Tim 2:7** says, And I have been chosen-this is the absolute truth-as a preacher and apostle to teach the gentiles about faith and truth.

It seems to me based on this scripture if they are not teaching faith and truth are they really chosen? Just a question.

Pastors should never back down from telling the truth.

Acts 20:19-21 says, I have done the Lord's work humbly-yes, and with tears. I have endured the trials that came to me from the plots of the Jews. Yet I never shrank from telling the truth, either publicly or in your homes, I have had one message for Jews and Gentiles alike-the necessity of turning from sin and turning to God, and of faith in our Lord Jesus.

I know you all have heard this before probably from your parents, "Do as I say, not as I do." Wow, but God does not think that way about his leaders, he wants them to practice what they preach.

Rom 2:21-23 says, Well, then if you teach others, why don't teach yourself? You tell others not to steal, but do you steal? You say it is wrong to commit adultery, but do you do it? You condemn idolatry, but do you steal from pagan temples? You are so proud of knowing the law, but dishonor God by breaking it.

God has plenty to say about his leaders from drinking, to their children, to being faithful to their wives and carrying themselves correctly. Really it's true.

1Tim Chapter 3 says, It is a true saying that if someone wants to be an elder, he desires an honorable responsibility, For an elder must be a man whose life cannot be spoken against. He must be faithful to his wife. He must exhibit self-control, live wisely, and have a good reputation, he must enjoy having guests in his home and must be able to teach. He must not be a heavy drinker or be violent. He must be gentle, peace loving, and not one who loves money. He must manage his own family well with children who respect and obey him. For if a man cannot manage his own household, how can he take care of God's church?

An elder must not be a new Christian, because he might be proud of being called so soon, and the devil will use that pride to make him fall. Also people outside the church must speak well of him so that he will not fall into the devil's trap and be disgraced.

In the same way deacons must be people who are respected and have integrity. They must not be heavy drinkers or greedy for money. They must be committed to the revealed truths of the Christian faith and must live with a clear conscience. Before they are appointed as deacons they should be given other responsibilities in the church as a test of their character and ability. If they do well, then they may serve as deacons.

In the same ways their wives must be respected and must not speak evil of others. They must exercise self-control and be faithful in everything they do.

A deacon must be faithful to his wife, and must be able to manage his children and household well. Those who do well as deacons will be rewarded with respect from others and will have increased confidence in their faith in Christ Jesus.

God wants his leaders to take care of his flock.

1Pet 5:2-4 says, Care for the flock of God entrusted to you. Watch over it willingly not grudgingly-not for what you will get out of it, but because you are eager to serve God. Don't Lord over the people assigned to your care, but lead them by your good example. And when the head shepherd comes, your reward will be never-ending share in his glory and honor.

Now we have covered what God expects from his Pastors and leaders, but He also expects things from the members concerning them.

We should treat then with respect.

1Cor 16:10-11 says, When Timothy comes treat him with respect. He is doing the Lord's work, just as I am. Don't let anyone despise him.

We should also take care of them, they should actually be paid. I have heard people say in the past, "they need to get a job." What do you think Pastoring is?

1Cor 9:7-10 says, What soldier has to pay his own expenses? And have you ever heard of a farmer who harvests his crop and doesn't have the right to eat some of it? What shepherd takes care of a flock of sheep and isn't allowed to drink some of the milk? And this isn't merely human opinion. Doesn't God's law say the same thing? For the law of Moses says, "Do not keep an ox from eating as it treads out the grain." Wasn't he speaking of us? Of course he was. Just as farm workers who plow fields and thresh the grain expect a share of the harvest, Christian workers should be paid by those they serve.

We should pray for our leadership.

1Tim 2:1-2 says, I urge you, first of all, to pray for all people. As you make your requests, plead for God's mercy upon them, and give thanks. Pray this way for kings and all others who are in authority, so that we can live in peace and quietness, in godliness and dignity?

We should also help them in ministry, they should not have to worry about the work of the ministry-because they need to study and teach the word of God.

Acts 6:2-4 says, So the twelve called a meeting of all the believers. "We apostles should spend our time preaching and teaching the word of God, not administering a food program," they said. "Now look around among yourselves, friends, and select seven men who are well respected and are full of the Holy Spirit and wisdom. We will put them in charge of this business. Then we can spend time in prayer and preaching and teaching the word."

Please understand leaders are not perfect, but God has a guideline for them in the word. Please leave room for forgiveness if there is a mistake made, but not a lifestyle of living wrong.

Be a blessing to the ministry that you become a part of. Be willing to help increase the Kingdom of God.

Help your Pastor and 1ˢᵗ Lady and work well with the leaders in place. Pray for them, respect them and give them honor. Amen

CHAPTER 13

"TITHES & OFFERING" (GIVING)

This is a very touching subject with some Christians, because this is dealing with their money and they have stuff to do with their money. I have heard people say that tithe is from the Old Testament and we live in the New Testament times. So, please tell me how the bills are to get paid at the church and ministries can meet the needs of the people without money? I'm waiting . . . Well, let's go to the word of God. There are several scriptures referring to tithes and offering in the Old and New Testament.

1Cor 16:2 says, On every Lord's Day, each of you should put aside some amount of money in relation to what you have earned and save it for this offering. Don't wait until I get there and then try to collect it all at one time.

Jesus says in this scripture that we should tithe and do ministry.

Luke 11:39-42 says, Then the Lord said to him, "You Pharisees are so careful to clean the outside of the cup and the dish, but inside you are still filthy-full of greed and wickedness! Fools! Didn't God make the inside as well as the outside? So give to the needy what you greedily possess, and you will be clean all over.

But how terrible it will be for you Pharisees! For you are careful to tithe even the tiniest part of your income, but you completely forget about justice and the love of God. You should tithe, yes, but you should not leave undone the more important things.

God wants us to give freely.

2Cor 8:3 says, For I can testify that they gave not only what they could afford but far more. And they did it of their own free will.

God wants us to give cheerfully.

2Cor 9:7-9 says, You must each make up your own mind as to how much you should give. Don't give reluctantly or in response to pressure. For God loves the person who gives cheerfully. And God will generously provide all you need. Then you will always have everything you need and plenty left over to share with others. As the Scriptures say, Godly people give generously to the poor. Their good deeds will never be forgotten.

The tithe is used to take care of the temple (church).

Mal 3:10 says, Bring all the tithes into the storehouse so there will be enough food in my Temple. If you do, says the Lord Almighty, "I will open the windows of heaven for you. I will pour out a blessing so great you won't have enough room to take it in! Try it! Let me prove it to you!

Know that God's ministry needs to be funded and if you receive an income, only 10 cent on a dollar is requested to make sure the ministry is covered financially. The administrator of the church can't go to the utility company and the bank and tell them Jesus paid it all. They have to pay with currency. God blesses you to be a blessing to His ministry. amen

CHAPTER 14

"BEWARE OF FALSE PROPHETS"

Just like there are ministries after God's own heart, there are some that are not. Some ministries teach the opposite of what God wants us to know and sometimes they are so close to the "truth" that it may trick you. Keep your eyes and ears open, because something will be revealed to let you know it's not a true ministry of God. Like some people say, "wrong spirit."

Now here is the word of God to explain what He thinks about them.

2Pet 2:1-3 says, But there were also false prophets in Israel, just as there will be false teachers among you. They will cleverly teach their destructive heresies about God and even turn against their Master who brought them. Theirs will be swift and terrible end. Many will follow their evil teaching and shameful immorality. And because of them, Christ and his true way will be slandered. In their greed they will make up clever lies to get hold of your money. But God condemned them long ago, and their destruction is on the way.

As you see God does not play about false prophets showing his sheep the wrong way. He is very serious about false prophets tricking his people.

The false prophets don't think about the consequences of their actions. They try to keep you from the truth. They also cause trouble and never stop trying to get rich.

1Tim 6:3-5 says, Some false teachers may deny these things, but these are the sound, wholesome teachings of the Lord Jesus Christ, and they are the foundation for a godly life. Anyone who teaches anything different is both conceited and ignorant. Such a person has an unhealthy desire to quibble over the meaning of words. This stirs up arguments ending in jealousy, fighting, slander and evil suspicions. These people always cause trouble. Their minds are corrupt, and they don't tell the truth. To them religion is just a way to get rich.

God will send judgment on false prophets.

Acts 13:4-12 says, Sent out by the Holy Spirit, Saul and Barnabas went down to the seaport of Seleucia and then sailed for the island of Cyprus. There, in the town of Salamis, they went to the Jewish synagogues and preached the word of God. (John Mark went with them as their assistant.)

Afterward they preached from town to town across the entire island until finally they reached Paphos, where they met a Jewish sorcerer, a false prophet named Bar-Jesus. He had attached himself to the governor, Serguis Paulus, a man of considerable insight and understanding. The governor invited Barnabas and Saul to visit him, for he wanted to hear the word of God. But Elymas, the sorcerer (as his name means in Greek), interfered and urged the governor away from the Christian faith. Then Saul, also known as Paul, filled with the Holy Spirit, looked the sorcerer in the eye and said, "You son of the devil, full of every sort of trickery and villiany, enemy of all that is good, will you never stop perverting the true ways of the Lord? And now the Lord has laid his hand of punishment upon you, and you will be stricken awhile with blindness."Instantly mist and darkness fell upon him, and he began wandering around begging for someone to take his hand and lead him. When the governor saw what had happened, he believed and was astonished at what he learned about the Lord.

As you see the false prophets do not want you know the full truth of the Lord, because it will set you free of the bondage of sin. It is not ok to be a

Christian and live in sin. God wants and has more for you and the devil knows that, so he will use whoever is a willing participate to lead you blindly like the sorcerer did, which if you think about it is "witchcraft."

There is still more warnings in God's word to false teaching.

1Tim 3-11 says, When I left for Macedonia, I urged you to stay there in Ephesus and stop those who are teaching wrong doctrine. Don't let people waste time in endless speculation over myths and spiritual pedigrees. For these things only cause arguments; they don't help people live a life of faith in God. The purpose of my instruction is that all Christians there would be filled with love that comes from a pure heart, clear conscience, and sincere faith.

But some teachers have missed this whole point. They have turned away from these things and spend their time arguing and talking foolishness. They want to be known as teachers of the law of Moses, but they don't know what they are talking about, even though they seem so confident. We know these laws are good when they are used as God intended. But they were not made for people who do what is right. They are for people who are disobedient and rebellious, who are ungodly and sinful, who consider nothing sacred and defile what is holy, who murder their father or mother or other people. These laws are for people who are sexually immoral, for homosexuals and slave traders, for liars and oath breakers, and for those who do anything else that contradicts the right teaching that comes from the glorious Good News entrusted to me by our blessed God.

God does not want you to encourage a false prophet in anyway.

2John 10-11 says, If someone comes to your meeting and does not teach the truth about Christ, don't invite him into your house or encourage him in any way. Anyone who encourages him becomes a partner in his evil work.

Wow, God does not play about his word. God said if you encourage him, for instance I have seen prophets come to churches and speak or teach and it was not of God and the other pastors in the audience and other people shouting to them, "that's some good word", "you better teach" and "get on the runway doc!" God is saying, if you are encouraging them, you are a partner in their evil work. Then you see afterwards they invite them to their house for dinner or out to eat. God says don't do that-wow!

There are some prophets that teach it's ok to live immoral lives-you are forgiven. Well, lets see what God words says about this.

Jude 4-9 says, I say this because some godless people have wormed their way in among you, saying that God's forgiveness allows us to live immoral lives. The fate of such people was determined long ago, for they have turned against our only Master and Lord, Jesus Christ.

I must remind you-and you know it well-that even though the Lord rescued the whole nation of Israel from Egypt, he later destroyed every one of those who did not remain faithful. And I remind you of the angels who did not stay within the limits of authority God gave them but left the place where they belonged. God has kept them chained in prisons of darkness, waiting for the Day of Judgment. And don't forget the cities of Sodom and Gomorrah and their neighboring towns, which were filled with sexually immorality and every kind of sexual perversions. Those cities were destroyed by fire and are a warning of the eternal fire that will punish all who are evil.

Yet these false teachers, who claim authority from their dreams, live immoral lives, defy authority, and scoff at the power of the glorious ones. But even Michael, one of the mightiest angels, did not dare accuse satan of blasphemy, but simply said, "The Lord rebuke you."

Please know that God is serious about this subject. He even tells us how to handle false prophets.

Rom 16:17-20 says, And now I make one more appeal, my dear brothers and sisters. Watch out for people who cause divisions and upset people's faith by teaching things that are contrary to what you have been taught. Stay away from them. Such people are not serving Christ our Lord; they are serving their own personal interests. By smooth talk and glowing words they deceive innocent people. But everyone knows that you are obedient to the Lord. This makes me very happy. I want you to see clearly what is right and to stay innocent of any wrong doing. The God of peace will soon crush satan under his feet. May the grace of our Lord Jesus Christ be with you.

He wants you to watch for this person and gives us plenty of clues to look for. Please pray about all things. If you have read this chapter and you have discovered you are under a false prophet, do what God's word says. Be lead to a Pastor that is teaching the word of God and described in God's word. Amen

CHAPTER 15

"DON'T BE MISLEAD"

While I was in the process of writing this book, I actually started studying this subject and that Sunday I went to church one of the ministers was teaching on being **mislead**-wow. Which just shows that God's people can be on one accord in the spirit.

When you start receiving God's word, which is the truth, don't let anyone or anything change your mind.

Col 1:23 says, But you must continue to believe this truth and stand in it firmly. Don't drift away from the assurance you received when you heard the Good News.

Don't let anyone just tell you anything and you believe it. Research God's word for the truth.

1Tim 1:3-4 says, When I left Macedonia, I urged you to stay there in Ephesus and stop those who are teaching wrong doctrine. Don't let people waste time in endless speculation over myths and spiritual pedigrees. For these things only cause arguments; they don't help people live a life of faith in God.

Don't believe lying spirits.

1Tim 4:1-2 says, Now the Holy Spirit tell us clearly that in the last times some will turn away from what we believe; they will follow lying spirits and teachings that come from demons. These teachers are hypocrites and liars. They pretend to be religious, but their consciences are dead.

Don't be fooled by what people say.

2Thess 2:1-3 says, And now, brothers and sisters, let us tell you about the coming again of our Lord Jesus Christ and how we will be gathered together to meet him. Please don't be easily shaken and troubled by those who say that the day of the Lord has already begun. Even if they claim to have had a vision, a revelation, or a letter supposedly from us, don't believe them. Don't be fooled by what they say.

Don't be like children believing whatever you are told, instead holdfast to the teachings of Jesus Christ.

Eph 4:14-16 says, Then we will no longer be like children, forever changing our minds about what we believe because someone has told us something different or because someone has cleverly lied to us and made the lie sound like the truth. Instead, we will hold to the truth in love, becoming more and more in every way like Christ, who is the head of his body, the church. Under his direction, the whole body is fitted together perfectly. As each part does its own special work, it helps the others grow, so that the whole body is healthy and growing and full of love.

Don't doubt about God's power.

Acts 10:38 says, And no doubt you know what God anointed Jesus of Nazareth with the Holy Spirit and with power. Then Jesus went around doing good and healing all who were oppressed by the devil, for God was with him.

Don't be **mislead** about what Jesus did for you.

Rom 8:1-4 says, So, now there is no condemnation for those who belong to Christ Jesus. For the power of the life-giving Spirit has freed you through

Christ Jesus from the power of sin that leads to death. The law of Moses could not save us, because of our sinful nature. But God put into effect a different plan to save us. He sent his own Son in a human body like ours, except that ours are sinful. God destroyed sin's control over us by giving his Son as sacrifice for our sins. He did this so that the requirement of the law would be fully accomplished for us who no longer follow the Spirit.

Don't be **mislead** that you can do anything you want to do and not be watchful.

Luke 21:34-36 says, Watch out! Don't let me find you living in careless ease and drunkenness, and filled with the worries of this life. Don't let that day catch you unaware, as in a trap. For that day will come upon everyone living on the earth. Keep a constant watch. And pray that, if possible, you may escape these horrors and stand before the Son of Man.

There has been several times I have been **mislead**, but when you learn better you do better. I have been **mislead** by leaders, friends, family and relationships.

Once you have been through something you should be able to quickly recognize someone is trying to **mislead** you, trick you, play you, run game on you, whichever line you want to use.

I attended a few churches for a very short time. Based on the teachings and the things that were being done-I knew instantly they were **misleading** their flock. I removed myself from the equation.

That includes friends also-for example: Someone I knew from the past saw me at the store and struck up conversation and was saying all the right things. He asked me on a date to the movies. At the time I was working on a play and writing books and he wanted to see me all the time, distracting me from my work for the Kingdom. One day we were walking in the park and he just ups and says he believes in God, but not Jesus. I was like what? Now for weeks he was talking about he has been thinking about me for years and always wanted to date me and he thought I was his soul mate. Now, you know I wanted to hear all of what he was saying right? I have been trying to live right waiting on the right "one". So, when he said that I was like are you serious? He went on to tell me why he believed in what he did. For a hot second I was confused, but never wavered from what I was taught. Everything he was saying, God had a scripture to back it up. I told him I believed God created everything and He sent his Son Jesus to die for my sins. Finally, within a couple of weeks I cut ties with him, no calling, texting or emailing. Because he was familiar to me, was nice looking and a gentleman-opening doors all that. But, he was trying to **mislead** me. Because of the things he was saying to me reached my ears into my spirit. I was up for several nights searching the scriptures. I could not argue with him because this was not a carnal fight, but a spiritual one, so I had to use the word of God in Jesus name. The devil had to flee.

2Cor 6:14-18 says, Don't team up with those who are unbelievers. How can goodness be a partner with wickedness? How can light live with darkness? What harmony can there be between Christ and the devil? How can a believer be a partner with an unbeliever? And what union can there be between God's temple and idols? For we are the temple of the living God. As God said: "I will live in them and walk among them. I will be their God, and they will be my people. Therefore, come out from them and separate yourselves from them, says the Lord. Don't touch their filthy things, and I will be your Father, and you will be my sons and daughters, says the Lord Almighty."

Stay alert and watchful. Amen-

CHAPTER 16

"RELATIONSHIPS"

God does not want us to be in any relationship resulting in sin of any kind. In order to grow spiritually you must avoid bad relationships or ungodly relationships.

A good relationship will motivate you to pursue the things of God. You must evaluate every relationship to determine if they are healthy or unhealthy for your spiritual growth (life). Even though you like someone does not mean they are good for you. The Bible says we should not associate with not only unbelievers that sin, but Christians that indulge in sin.

1Cor 5:9-13 says, When I wrote to you before, I told you not to associate with people who indulge in sexual sin. But I wasn't talking about unbelievers who indulge in sexual sin, or who are greedy or are swindlers or idol worshipers. You would have to leave this world to avoid people like that. What I mean was that you are not to associate with anyone who claims to be a Christian yet indulges in sexual sin, or is greedy, or worship idols or is abusive or a drunkard or a swindler. Don't even eat with such people.

It isn't my responsibility to judge outsiders, but it certainly is your job to judge those inside the church who are sinning in these ways. God will judge those on the outside; but as the Scriptures say, "You must remove the evil person from among you."

God doesn't want us to be in any relationship with sexual sin-our body is a temple.

1Cor 6:9-10 says, Don't you know that those who do wrong will have no share in the Kingdom of God? Don't fool yourselves. Those who indulge in sexual sin, who are idol worshipers, adulterers, male prostitutes, homosexuals, thieves, greedy people, drunkards, abusers, and swindlers-none of these will have a share in the Kingdom of God.

1Cor 6:15-20 says, Don't you realize that your bodies are actually parts of Christ? Should a man take his body, which belongs to Christ and join it to a prostitute? Never! And don't you know that if a man joins himself to a prostitute, he becomes one body with her? For the Scriptures say, "The two are united into one." But the person who is joined to the Lord becomes one spirit with him.

Run away from sexual sin! No other sin so clearly affects the body as this one does. For sexual immorality is a sin against your own body. Or don't you know that your body is the temple of the Holy Spirit, who lives in you and was given to you by God? You do not belong to yourself, for God bought you with a high price. So you must honor God with your body.

Relationships as far as "dating" is concerned it should be done decent and in order. I was told by a very wise person before that we are considered to be God's children, so that makes women and men-brothers and sisters in Christ right? Well, we should only think of each other as brothers and sisters in Christ and treat each other as such, until a determination is made for engagement or marriage.

We definitely don't want to keep spending time together dating and our emotions and desires start getting the best of us. Well guess what God wants us to get married-not shack or have a sexual relationship even if it is potential husband or wife and even if he has a "ring on it".

1Cor 7:36 says, But if a man thinks he ought to marry his fiancée' because he has trouble controlling his passions and time is passing, it is all right; it is not a sin. Let them marry.

God does not want us in relationships that will take us away from Him.

1Cor 7:35 says, I am saying this for your benefit, not to place restrictions on you. I want you to do whatever will help you serve the Lord best, with as few distractions as possible.

Relationships as far as "husband and wives" gets a little more in depth. God expects you to treat each other in a Godly manner. I think this relationship would last longer and be more fulfilling if they followed God's word.

1Pet 3:7 says, In the same way, you husbands must give honor to your wives. Treat her with understanding as you live together. She may be weaker than you are, but she is your equal partner in God's gift of new life. If you don't treat her as you should, your prayers will not be heard.

1Pet 3:1-5 says, In the same way, you wives must accept the authority of your husbands, even those who refuse to accept the Good News. Your godly lives will speak to them better than any words. They will be won over by watching your pure, godly behavior.

Don't be concerned about the outward beauty that depends on fancy hairstyles, expensive jewelry or beautiful clothes. You should be known for the beauty that comes from within, the unfading beauty of a gentle and quiet spirit, which is so precious to God. That is the way the holy women of old made themselves beautiful.

I have spoken with a lot of wives that complain how their husbands treat them. They feel like the relationship is one-sided and the husband wants what he wants and that is it. Also they think when the Bible says they are the "head" of the wife-the husband takes it literally and Lord's over them. God's word says different. He wants the marriage relationship to be a loving and kind partnership. God wants the husband and wife to love, honor and respect one another.

Eph 5:21-31 says, And further, you will submit to one another out of reverence for Christ. You wives will submit to your husbands as you do to the Lord. For a husband is the head of his wife as Christ is the head of his body, the church; gave his life to be her Savior: As the church submits to Christ, so you wives must submit to your husbands in everything.

And you husbands must love your wives with the same love Christ showed the church. He gave up his life for her to make her holy and clean, washed by baptism and God's word. He did this to present her to himself as a glorious church without a spot or wrinkle or any other blemish. Instead she will be holy, and without fault. In the same way, husbands ought to love their wives as they love their own bodies. For a man is actually loving himself when he loves his wife. No one hates his own body but lovingly cares for it, just as Christ cares for his body, which is the church. And we are his body.

As the Scriptures say, "A man leaves his father and mother and is joined to his wife, and the two are united into one."

Relationships concerning "Parents and Children"—God wants us as parents to love our children and teach them what is right and we shouldn't do things to them just for spite. We should nurture them.

Prov 22:6 says, Teach your children to choose the right path, and when they are older, they will remain upon it.

Prov 19:18 says, Discipline your children while there is hope. If you don't, you will ruin their lives.

Prov 15:5 says, Only a fool despises a parent's discipline; whoever learns from correction is wise.

Eph 6:1-4 says, Children obey your parents because you belong to the Lord, for this is the right thing to do. Honor your father and mother. This is the first of the Ten Commandments that ends with a promise: If you honor your father and mother. You will live a long life, full of blessing.

And now a word to you fathers. Don't make your children angry by the way you treat them. Rather bring them up with the discipline and instruction approved by the Lord.

Parents, we are to teach our children to love God and show them the way.

Deut 6:6-7 says, And you must commit yourselves wholeheartedly to those commands I am giving you today. Repeat them again and again to your children. Talk about them when you are at home and when you are away on a journey, when you are lying down and when you are getting up again.

The Bible says if you don't discipline your children you don't love them.

Prov 13:24 says, if you refuse to discipline your children, it proves you don't love them; if you love your children, you will be **prompt** to discipline them.

Children should obey their parents. Meaning parents do not let your children disobey you. Set rules that should be followed-if not see previous scriptures.

Col 3:20 says, You children must always obey your parents.

God is serious about children honoring their parents he put it in the Ten Commandments.

Deut 5:16 says, Honor your father and mother, as the Lord your God commanded you. Then you will live a long, full life in the land the Lord your God will give you.

The relationship concerning "God and youth"—God doesn't want the excitement of being young, let you forget about him.

Eccl 12:1-2 says, Don't let the excitement of youth cause you to forget your Creator. Honor him in your youth before you grow old and no longer enjoy living. It will be too late then to remember him, when the light of the sun and moon and stars is dim to your old eyes.

While you are still young start doing ministry for God and keep your mind on building the Kingdom of God. Don't think you have so much time because you are young. You can enjoy your youth, but keep God first.

Relationships concerning "friends"—God says a friend should be loyal and not be around you just for your money.

Prov 17:17 says, A friend is always loyal, a brother born to help in time of need.

Prov 18:24 says, There are 'friends' who destroy each other, but a real friend sticks closer than a brother.

Prov 19:4 says, Wealth makes many"friends", poverty drives them away.

I remember one time I got a settlement. I had so many friends my house almost couldn't hold them. Every Sunday after church for about a month everybody was at my house for dinner. But when the funds got low-I couldn't find a friend with a flashlight.

Relationships concerning "employers and employees"—God wants us as employees to respect our supervisor, manager, boss-whatever the title. We should follow directions and carry out our duties without an attitude and with a servant's heart. I have been on both sides and have not always approached every situation correctly, but you live and you learn.

God also expects employers to treat their employees right as well.

The Bible refers to employers as masters and the employees as slaves. Which is actually reality, so don't get mad.

Eccl 9:10 says, Whatever you do, do well. For when you go to the grave, there will be no work or planning or knowledge or wisdom.

Eph 6:5-9 says, Slaves, obey your earthly masters with deep respect and fear. Serve them sincerely as you would serve Christ. Work hard, but not just to please your masters when they are watching. As slaves of Christ, do the will of God with all your heart. Work with enthusiasm, as though you were working for the Lord rather than for people. Remember that the Lord will reward each of us for the good we do, whether we are slaves or free.

And in the same way, you masters must treat your slaves right. Don't threaten them; remember you both have the same Master in Heaven, and he has no favorites.

The Bible lets us know that in relationships whether husband-wife, parent-child, dating, friendships or employment. God wants us to treat each other right. We should study the word of God to continue to know how to treat one another in all relationships! amen

CHAPTER 17

"HEALING"

Healing means to restore to good health.

No matter how hard you try to be in perfect health sometimes you get sick. A lot of times we depend on the doctor to cure us. God loves us and he is not limited to only working through doctors.

God is a healer and he sent his Son Jesus Christ to show his healing power. Jesus healed so many in the Bible and He is still in the healing business today. Jesus healed in so many ways, but you have to believe-meaning have faith that you will be healed.

Matt 9:18 says, Jesus was saying this, the leader of a synagogue came and knelt down before him. "My daughter has just died, "he said, but you can bring her back to life again if you just come and lay your hand upon her.

Matt 9:23-26 says, When Jesus arrived at the official's home, he noticed the noisy crowds and heard funeral music. He said, "go away, for the girl isn't dead; she's only asleep." But the crowd laughed at him. When the crowd was finally outside, Jesus went in and took the girl by the hand and she stood up! The report of this miracle swept through the entire countryside.

Sometimes you have to respond in faith with your words.

Matt 9:27-29 says, After Jesus left the girl's home, two blind men followed along behind him, shouting "Son of David, have mercy on us!" They went right into the house where he was staying and Jesus asked them, "Do you believe I can make you see?" "Yes, Lord," they told him, "we do." Then he touched their eyes and said, "Because of your faith, it will happen." And suddenly they could see! Jesus sternly warned them, "Don't tell anyone about this."

You need to be free of **un-repented** sin for healing power.

Mark 6:12 says, So the disciples went out, telling all they met to turn from sins. And they cast out many demons and healed many sick people, anointing them with olive oil.

You have to have faith and be determined don't let anything stop you from your healing.

Luke 5:18-21 says, Some men came carrying a paralyzed man on a sleeping mat. They tried to push through the crowd to Jesus, but they couldn't reach him. So they went up to the roof, took off some tiles and lowered the sick man down into the crowd, still on his mat, right in front of Jesus, "Son your sins are forgiven."

Luke 5:24-25 says, "I will prove that I, the Son of Man, have the authority on earth to forgive sins." Then Jesus turned to the paralyzed man and said, "Stand up, take your mat, and go on home, because you are healed!" And immediately, as everyone watched, the man jumped to his feet, picked up his mat, and went home praising God.

You are unable to get your blessing or miracle if don't believe you can be healed.

Matt 13:58 says, And so he did only a few miracles there because of their unbelief.

What do I do if I get sick and want someone to pray for me? One suggestion would be call the elders of the church. Remember confess your sins, ask for forgiveness also.

Jam 5:14-16 says, Are any among you sick? They should call the elders of the church and have them pray over them, anointing them with oil in the name of the Lord. And their prayer offered in faith will heal the sick and the Lord will make them well. And anyone who has committed sins will be forgiven. Confess your sins to each other and pray for each other so that you may be healed. The earnest prayer of a righteous person has great power and wonderful result.

Jesus healed in several ways in the Bible, some by laying hands or even just speaking into their lives, but they had to have faith and believe that they would be healed and receive forgiveness for their sins.

God has healed me in so many ways and he is healing me right now. I just had a procedure done and the only thing that is healing me is Jesus. The doctors' did what they could and the rest is left up to God.

When I first became a Christian I didn't have a lot of faith and children are different, when they hear the word of God somehow they grasp it and believe more than their parents do. Well, when my son was like in the 1ˢᵗ grade, I was diagnosed with lupus. I was distraught and just crying and my son said "what's wrong momma?" I explained that I had lupus and I might die soon and he could live with his grandmother. He looked at me with those big brown eyes and said, "Momma, I am going to pray for you." Now he is in the 1ˢᵗ grade, but we had just started going to church a lot. He was on the bed and he put his hands on me and said something like this, "God please heal my momma-I need her and I love my momma, please don't take her away from me, don't let her die God" I just cried and he hugged me and said, "Don't cry momma."

I went back to the doctor the next week and they said my lupus was gone. Now don't tell me what God won't do, because I will tell you what He can do-amen!

Years ago, I was at church one day and we had a visiting Pastor and he told us to get in the aisle and dance for God, give Him some praise and I guess I must have been dancing harder than anybody else, because he told the men to bring me to him and when I got to him he put his hand on my head and told me I was healed. I blacked out and when I woke up-people were standing over me praying. Well, I didn't know I needed to be healed until the next day or so, I got what I thought was "ill". I was almost like the woman in the Bible with the "issue of blood", my friend rushed me to the hospital, because it was so much blood I thought I was going to die. But guess what-I was sick in my body and didn't know it and God was cleansing my body. Blood clots that had set up in my body were coming out and God healed me when I didn't even know I needed to be healed. God is all knowing and all powerful!

Please know that God can do it! Keep the faith and stay in God's word pertaining to your healing!

CHAPTER 18

"FORGIVENESS"

Forgive means to pardon or cease to feel resentment.

So, when you forgive someone you let it go. Whatever they did to you or even how they made you feel should be forgiven. You must release them from your heart, mind and spirit. Because you know when someone hurts you, usually you think about it over and over. Thinking about what they said, how they said it, what they did, how they did it and what you should have done, but you have to let that go.

When I said let them go in your heart, well because we have feelings and people tend to say you broke my heart when you said that or did that. They have songs about your achy, breaky heart. But let it go.

And when I said let them go in your spirit. I am sure you have heard people say, "When she left him, she just broke his spirit." But you have to let it go.

I am going to let God's word reveal itself. We have to forgive others to be forgiven by God. Really? Yes, really. You have heard people say, "I will never forgive them!" Well, let's think about that shall we.

I would rather forgive others so God can forgive me and bless me.

God is just and ready to forgive us.

Psalm 86:5 says, O Lord, you are so good, so ready to forgive, so fully unfailing love for all who ask your aid.

Matt 6:12 says, And forgive us our sins, just as we have forgiven those who have sinned against us.

Matt 6:14-15 says, If you forgive those who sin against you, your Heavenly Father will forgive you. But, if you refuse to forgive others, your Father will not forgive your sins.

I do not want to be that guy that is not forgiven. You may want to think back and make sure you are not holding un-forgiveness for anyone. Because it holds you back spiritually.

I love my mother, but I felt like she could have done more, said more, was around more, when I was younger. But, she had to deal with a lot of issues with my older brothers and her own life issues. I was the youngest and I felt alone a lot and that there should have been more family interaction.

I really didn't realize I felt that way, because I was like in my 30's. Until one night I was in Women's Ministry and I can't actually remember the subject matter, but it had to do something with mothers or families. Well, I made a little joke as usually, which I found out later the jokes were to mask my hurt. But, all of a sudden I started crying, I mean seriously crying. The 1ˢᵗ Lady dismissed the class at once, so she could talk to me. As the discussion grew, she explained to me that my mom did what she knew how to do. She told me that I had to think about if my mom had mentors or if her mother taught her how to take care of kids. She said my mom did the best she knew how. The more she talked the more I realized that I was holding un-forgiveness towards my mother. I had to forgive her and as soon as I did, I felt a burden lift off of me.

I know I have probably said or done something my son didn't like or thought I could have done better about. We all have to learn to forgive and treat that person how you want to be treated. At one time or another, we have been that person that forgave or was forgiven.

What if someone sins against you over and over?

Matt 18:21-22 says, Then Peter came to him and asked, "Lord how often should I forgive someone who sins against me? Seven times? "No!" Jesus replied, "Seventy times seven!" Meaning every time regardless of how many times.

You know how we get offended. We all do it one time or another. You have people that see all your faults, but not their own. God's word will take care of each person individually. If someone offends me I have to forgive them regardless if they see their fault or not.

Col 3:13 says, You must make allowances for each other's faults and forgive the person who offends you. Remember, the Lord forgave you, so you must forgive others.

Make sure you forgive others in the right spirit. Meaning not with an attitude or unwilling heart. Amen

Wow! I have come across a few people like this. They feel everybody else has sin or fault, but them. They can even call yours out in front other people or even in a whisper to others. I could never understand if someone calls you a "gossiper", but they are talking about you to other people—saying you are a "gossiper." But what does that make them, "hello!'

God is working on us until the day of Jesus return. No sin is greater than another.

1John 1:8-10 says, If we say we have no sin, we are only fooling ourselves and refusing to accept the truth. But if we confess our sins to him, he is faithful and just to forgive us and to cleanse us from every wrong.

If we claim we have not sinned, we are calling God a liar and showing that his word has no place in our hearts.

Please be true to thyself. God wants us to forgive our enemies, which we think is hard.

Matt 5:44 says, But I say, love your enemies! Pray for those who persecute you. In that way you will be acting as children of your Father in Heaven. You have to forgive them to love them.

Forgive yourself, forgive others and ask God to forgive you!

Walk in forgiveness everyday life from someone cutting you off in the traffic, breaking in front of you in line or stepping on your foot. FORGIVE! Amen!

CHAPTER 19

"BEING A WITNESS"

Witnessing is a being a witness to something you know to be true, because you experienced it or saw it in person.

For instance, when an accident happens the police look for a witness at the scene. So, they can give their version of the events that occurred.

God would like for us to be a witness for Him. He wants us to tell people what we have seen, what we have experienced or our encounters with Him and His Son Jesus Christ.

As you develop a personal relationship with our Father—you will find He will give you strength through hard times and will show you love through others. As you experience His unconditional love, God wants you to share those events.

I know you think you are special and you are, but God loves everyone and He wants you to share Him with others and not keep Him all to yourself. That would be selfish. Jesus died to save everyone and He wants a relationship with them too.

First make sure you have a good attitude and you are letting the love of Jesus shine through you daily. Who wants to listen to someone with a bad attitude tell them about Jesus? Not me and anyone that I know.

We witness through our words and actions toward the unsaved, lost and un-churched.

Every person is different and in a different place in their lives. You may not witness to each person the same. What you said to help Beverly might not help Sam, so you have to let the Holy Spirit lead you in witnessing and giving the person you are witnessing to what they need at the time.

For instance, I went to the library café, I was starving. I saw the person behind the counter looked frustrated. There was a child at the counter making a purchase. The Holy Spirit instantly brought to my mind that she was not having a good day, so I decided to let my light shine even though I was having a similar day. When it was my turn to order, I asked her how she was doing and were the kids working her nerves today-because school was out? She went into how many kids were coming to the café over and over, because their parents gave them twenty-dollars and they were wearing her out. She continued telling me about her day and she was tired etc. I listened and responded in the love of Christ. During our short conversation I told her it would be ok and some people didn't have jobs and God is still good. We continued our conversation while she made my sandwich and she said she was so glad that I came by, because she needed that encouragement at that time.

What is so funny is the library was not the intended place I was going to get something to eat. A few minutes prior I was at a local eatery and the service was not good so I walked out before ordering and my son told me weeks ago about the café in the library and since I was going to work on my book I decided to eat there. You see how the Holy Spirit works, He sent me there at that moment to witness and encourage her. We have to be obedient to the Holy Spirit and be ready to witness even when our day is going bad. By me lifting her spirits I lifted mine at the same time. God is just good like that!

You can witness anywhere or anytime. For example: you go to the grocery store a couple of times a week and when get to the cashier to check out, you speak and ask them how they are doing and always with a good attitude-remember they are serving you. When they give you your change you might say, "Thank you and God bless you" or "Thank you have a blessed day."

Then one day they ask you, "Why are you so happy all the time?" Bingo-good opportunity to witness. You don't have to give a "sermon" to spread the Good News. You could simply say, "God has been good to me" or "God is so good, I just can't tell it all" or "Jesus loves me and you too."

If the conversation continues, or If not, you have just planted a seed. You might not be the person to lead in the word of salvation passage, but you have done your part at this point. More opportunities may arise and please be ready and willing to respond appropriately.

1Cor 3:6 says, I planted the seed, Apollos watered it, but God made it grow.

Don't be afraid to open your mouth and spread the "Good News" or tell people about Jesus and what He has done for you.

Acts 1:8 says, But you will receive power when the Holy Spirit comes on you and you will be my witnesses in Jerusalem and in all Judea and Samaria and to the ends of the earth.

We as Christians are considered disciples of Jesus Christ. Jesus wants disciples to make disciples. Almost like an army recruits for soldiers. They send out other soldiers that have experienced the army. They are the best people to recruit, because they know the benefits of being in the army and the knowledge to answer the potential soldiers' questions. They can also tell them why they made the choice to be in the army. Which is what "witnessing" is all about.

We should always be ready and willing to respond.

1Pet 3:15 says, But in your hearts set apart Christ as Lord. Always be prepared to give an answer to everyone who asks you to give the reason for the hope that you have.

Please understand there are some people including man, woman and child, that have never read a Bible and have no knowledge of God and they are lost. They've never been to church or associate with any Christians.

That is why it is important to show the love of Christ. Showing the love of Christ definitely makes people notice there is something special about you.

You could meet a "potential" Christian in any number of places like: grocery store, post office, bus stop, the list goes on. But never let your chance pass to witness to someone about the "true light" which is the realization of Jesus Christ. Remember someone took the time to do it for you.

Witnessing consists of a number of approaches, remember you need to consider where the person is in their life. Someone may have already planted a seed and when they get to you, they might say, "I know about Jesus, but I need to get back in church and get my life right."

You have the opportunity to tell them that God never stopped loving them. You could ask them if they were saved and if not lead them into the salvation prayer. If they said they are a Christian but have been living a sinful life. Let them know Jesus died for their sins and all they have to do is ask Him for forgiveness and He will be just to forgive.

You can also invite them to church-which is a part of witnessing. For instance if they say, "I don't have a church home" or "I used to go to church." There is an opening to invite them to church.

Once you invite them to church make sure they have a ride, if not make provisions for them to get there. If your church provides bus services-contact that ministry and make sure they are picked up for church. If the decision is made that they are going to need an alternative ride, please let the Holy Spirit lead you. If the person is of the opposite gender, have a member of the same gender to escort them to church. We want to be decent and in order even in bringing people to church and we want to be safe.

Like I said before everybody is not saved or delivered from everything, so you still have to be sober minded in the world we live in. amen

If you do reach someone that says, "Yes, I am ready to be a Christian and be a part of God's Kingdom".

Ask them if they believe what **John 3:16** says, God so loved the world that He gave His one and only Son (Jesus Christ) that whoever believes in Him shall not perish but have eternal life.

Also, lead them in the Salvation prayer. Some say it a little different from others, but as long as it is understood that forgiveness is asked for and received and their heart has turned to God. Here is an example (ask them to repeat after you):

Dear Jesus, I know I've done wrong things. I've made a lot of mistakes. The Bible calls what I've done a sin. I understand you love me so much you died on a cross for my sins. I understand you didn't stay dead, but you rose from the grave after three days. If you can defeat death, I believe you can help me defeat sin in my life. I invite you into my life right now. I put my trust in you. I believe your death on the cross was payment for my sins. Help me to learn and live for you. Amen

Understand you don't have to be a Pastor to tell people about Jesus. Actually, being witnesses we should bring others to church so that our Pastor can Minister to them the word of God. You don't have to have a degree or special skills to help build the Kingdom of God. You simply need to be willing to tell someone about Jesus.

We meet people every day that need God's love and forgiveness. It is our responsibility to share the gift of Salvation.

Luke 15:10 says, "There's rejoicing in the presence of the angels of God over one sinner who repents."

God bless you and stay in the word of God to increase your knowledge. Always be prepared to witness through our actions, words and lifestyles. Amen

CHAPTER 20

"MINISTRY"

I know when you hear ministry you think of the Minister or Pastor, but it actually means the act of serving. It's not just a Pastor's job, but the responsibility of all Christians to serve in the ministry.

As you grow close to God through prayer, worship and reading God's word- you will gain knowledge and wisdom from God. During this time you will become stronger as a Christian spiritually. Because you are stronger spiritually you are able to serve through ministry effectively.

In ministry the more time you spend with God the more successful you will be in serving.

God wants us to minister through serving. God sent his Son Jesus to show us how to serve. He was a great example to show us how to minister with a "servant's heart", which means you have to be unselfish and have humility.

Once you give your heart to Christ, He expects you to follow in His footsteps. He wants you to place more importance on others than yourself.

You should start with a clean heart. You should not have wrong motives, but have the heart and attitude of Jesus-thinking of others above self. Have you have heard the phrase, "WWJD-What Would Jesus Do?" Sometimes you have to take a moment to think on that level instead of your own.

Humility is the opposite of self-importance. Meaning putting others first. God wants us to love in humility toward others. He wants you to see them more important than ourselves, which is having attitude of a servant-that is exactly what God wants from us.

In **Luke 22:27**, which took place during the Last Supper. Jesus asked his disciples who was better. One who sat at the table or the one who serves. Like the disciples many of us think the one who sits at the table more important because he is being served, but Jesus said, "But I am among you as one who serves." And then, to show His disciples that he also serves, he washed their feet (in those days washing feet was a lowly task). Jesus did this to show his disciples how much He loves them and to call them to serve one another in humility. Jesus also wants his disciples to love one another as he does.

John 13:34-35 says, "A command I give you; Love one another, as I have loved you. So, you must love one another by this all men will know that you are my disciples, if you love one another." You are also showing the love of Jesus when you serve.

You can serve in a lot of different ways, you can start in your church and in your community.

For example, if you like children, volunteer to work in the nursery or a youth program. To me there is "in-reach" and "out-reach."

In-reach means ministering in your church through cleaning, volunteering in classes, participating in programs, serving in different ministries within your church.

Out-reach means ministering to serve your community. For instance, having clothes give-a-ways, food drives, feeding the hungry, visiting the shut-in, visiting jails, visiting nursing homes, having carnivals for kids outreach to bring kids to Christ and the list can go on.

I think we should participate and serve in both an "in-reach" and "out-reach", ministering in church and the community.

There is so much for us to do for God's Kingdom and so many to reach. All of us need to participate.

Matt 9:37 says, Then he said to the disciples, "The harvest is plentiful but the workers are few." Meaning there is many people to reach, but few Christians that are participating in ministry.

Jesus want us to do a greater work than he did and he did a lot.

John 14:12 says, "The truth is, anyone who believes in me will do the same works I have done, and even greater works, because I am going to be with my Father."

You may feel shy or just don't know where to start. Even if you don't know where to start, start somewhere-just don't sit down on God.

When I first started church years ago-I didn't know where to start either. I've always liked children even when I was a kid. I used to babysit and loved doing their hair, keeping them clean, reading books to them etc. I remember even volunteering at my son's school on Fridays. I would bring pizza or cookies and read the class funny books. The children loved it and couldn't wait until the next Friday.

All of this never crossed my mind when I first started church, but the First Lady of the church was watching me. She noticed how I reacted around children and how they would respond to me by surrounding me and would love on me while I loved on them (meaning hugging, talking to them, encouraging them etc.).

So, one day we had a lock-in for the girls and she put me over a group of girls. I was so nervous, but once the night was over-I had the same count I started with, which means I didn't lose anybody or no one came up missing. I was sleepy and tired, but happy, because I laughed and played with then all night. As some of them fell asleep, several remained up and wanted to talk. They were telling me their problems at home and school, also how they felt as a person.

As I listened in love and responded in the same, they told me how much they appreciated me and loved me. I told them that God loved them and He would never leave them. I gave more advice as if I were in their shoes. They thanked me for listening to them and wanted me to continue being there for them. God used me in ministry to serve those girls.

From that night grew into me helping in classes and programs to being over or the leader of several ministries and getting programs accomplished from beginning through completion.

So, let God use you as a servant to serve one another through ministry. Once you get involved you will find your gifts and talents.

I have served through cleaning the church, ushering, security, teaching classes (children & adults), children ministry, outreach ministry, Christian stand-up comedy, teaching dance, teaching songs in sign language, contact ministry, reading books to kids on Saturdays at the church, helping build houses with Habitat for Humanity, cooking and serving food, doing fundraisers for the kid's choir, mentoring, plays, and more including writing books.

Please let God direct your path! Find a place in ministry to serve with a servant's heart.

God bless you and be a blessing!

CHAPTER 21

"SPIRITUAL GIFTS"

Spiritual Gifts are God given abilities for ministering. I have been taught there are 23 different Spiritual Gifts listed in the New Testament. These Spiritual Gifts are given for a Spiritual purpose.

We are given different Spiritual Gifts but for one purpose to edify (serve) the body of Christ.

1Cor 12:5 says, "There are different kinds of service in the church but it is the same God we are serving."

Why do we have Spiritual Gifts?

1Cor 12:7 says, A Spiritual Gift is given to each of us as a means of helping the entire church.

What are some of the Spiritual Gifts?

1Cor 12:8-10 says, To one person the Spirit gives the ability to give wise advise; to another he gives the gift of special knowledge. The Spirit gives special faith to another, and to someone else he gives the power to heal the sick. He gives one person the power to perform miracles, and to another the ability to prophesy. He gives another the ability to know whether it is really the Spirit of God or another spirit that is speaking. Still another person is given the ability to speak in "unknown languages," and another is given the ability to interpret what is being said.

How is it determined what Spiritual Gift I receive?

1Cor 12:11 says, It is the one and only Holy Spirit who distributes these gifts. He alone decides which gift each person should have.

God works through us by our gifts.

1Cor 12:6 says, There are different ways God work in our lives, but it is the same God who does the work through all of us.

Remember Spiritual Gifts are reserved for the Saints. You can't receive the gifts of the Spirit until you receive the gift of the Spirit which is Salvation.

Non-believers are not spiritually gifted. They may be talented but God reserved Spiritual gifts for Christians.

1Cor 2:12-15 says, And God has actually given us His Spirit (not the world's spirit) so we can know the wonderful things God has freely given us. When we tell you this, we do not use word of human wisdom. We speak words given to us by the Spirit, using the Spirit's words to explain spiritual truths. But people who aren't Christians can't understand these truths from God's Spirit. It all sounds foolish to them because only those who have the Spirit can understand what the Spirit means. We who have the Spirit understand these things, but others can't understand us at all.

It is our responsibility to discover our own gifts and use them to help encourage our brothers and sisters in Christ. This also includes ministry tasks and building up the body of Christ.

Please pray and ask God to reveal your gifts. Once the Holy Spirit reveals them, you should sharpen your gifts so that our Father will be glorified through them.

Here is a list of some Spiritual gifts:

Administrations	—	1 Corinthians 12:28-30
Apostle	—	1 Corinthians 12:28-30
Discerning of Spirits	—	Corinthians 12:8-10
Evangelism	—	Ephesians 4:11
Exhortation	—	Romans 12:6-8
Faith	—	1 Corinthians 12:8-10
Giving	—	Romans 12:6-8
Healing	—	1 Corinthians 12:28-30
Help	—	1 Corinthians 12:28
Hospitality	—	Romans 12:9-13
Interpretation of Tongues	—	1 Corinthians 12:28-30
Knowledge	—	1 Corinthians 12:28-30
Leadership	—	Romans 12:6-8
Miracles	—	1 Corinthians 12:8-10, 28-30
Mercy	—	Romans 12:6-8
Pastor	—	Ephesians 4:11
Teacher	—	Ephesians 4:11, Romans 12:7
Tongues	—	1 Corinthians 12:6-8, 23-30
Wisdom	—	1 Corinthians 12:8-10
Prophecy	—	1 Corinthians 12:6-8, 12:8-10, 28-30
Serving	—	Romans 12:6-8, 1 Peter 4:8-11
Teaching	—	Romans 12:6-8, 1 Corinthians 12:28-30
Speaking in Tongues	—	1 Peter 4:8-11

God bless you and help your church grow spiritually!

CHAPTER 22

"THE RAPTURE"

Going to church, watching television and being around other Christians you may have heard the word "rapture." The word rapture means to catch away. The word rapture does not appear in the Bible, but it is used to describe the event in which Christ will descend from Heaven and all those who have been saved will rise to meet him in the air.

1 Thess 4:16-18 says, "For the Lord himself will come down from Heaven, with a loud commanding shout, with the call of the archangel, and with the trumpet call of God. First, all the Christians who have died will rise from their graves. Then together with them, we who are still alive and remain on the earth will be caught up in the clouds to meet the Lord in the air and remain with him forever. So comfort and encourage each other with these words.

When we go to be with Jesus, every believer living or dead, will get a new body, one that will never die.

1Cor 15:51-54 says, But let me tell you a wonderful secret God has revealed to us. Not all of us will die, but we will all be transformed. It will happen in a moment, in the blinking of an eye, when the last trumpet is blown. For when the trumpet sounds, the Christians who have died will be raised with transformed bodies. And then we who are living will be transformed so that we will never die. For our perishable earthly bodies, must be transformed into heavenly bodies that will never die. When this happens-when our perishable earthly bodies have been transformed into heavenly bodies that will never die-then at last Scriptures will come true: "Death is swallowed up in victory."

The rapture will occur in an instant-in the "twinkling of an eye." How fast is the twinkling of an eye? It has been described has a "blink" of an eye and that is fast. When the rapture occurs Christians will instantly leave this earth and be in Heaven with Jesus.

You must be all so ready, meaning you must always be ready to go to Heaven because the Bible says that no man knows when the rapture will take place.

Matt 24:36 says, "However no man knows the day or the hour when these things will happen, not even angels in Heaven nor the Son himself, but only the Father knows."

God is waiting for his children to come home and he has prepared so much for us in Heaven. **John 14:2-3** says, In my Father's house are many rooms; if it were not so, I would tell you plainly. When everything is ready, I will come and get you, so that you will always be with me where I am. And you know where I am going and how to get there.

When we get to Heaven, we will have only joy, no sorrow, pain or death. Jesus is coming back to take the faithful home (Heaven).

If the rapture happened right now, would you be leaving with Jesus?

Also, read **Revelation Chapters 20-22**

CHAPTER 23

"STAY ENCOURAGED"

Please stay encouraged in Jesus Christ and don't let this world discourage you from doing what is right by God's word! Here's a few things that can help:

1. Read your Bible, good books, listen to spiritual music: Daily Bible reading will increase your faith. Your local Christian bookstore has an excellent selection of books, dvds, music, games and more to help you learn the principles of the Kingdom of God.

2. Find a Ministry (Church home): every Christian should find a place of ministry in order to serve in ministry and be ministered to. Whether you serve as an usher, greeter, children's church volunteer, or bus driver, find a place to serve! This will help you meet other people and keep you connected to your church.

3. Find a Mentor: you should always have someone in your Christian life, who can challenge and encourage you in building a relationship with God. Look for someone that has been a Christian longer than you and you have watched them

and respect them in what they are doing for the Kingdom of God. Ask them to help you learn more about Jesus and what it means to be a Christian. Also, they may be able to help guide you in perfecting your gifts and talents.

4. Be committed to your local church: Wisdom is power against the enemy, attend every service every week when possible we all know things come up, but make sure you keep God first and you learn what God has for you. When you attend church you connect with God and others in the ministry. We need to be with other Christians to build up and encourage one another!

5. Don't give up! We all make mistakes even Christians. If you make a mistake and sin-just ask God to forgive you and decide not to make that mistake again. The same way God forgave all yours sins when you became a Christian, he'll forgive them every time you ask. God never promised us a worry free life or a mistake free life. However, he did promise He would never leave or forsake us. When times get hard remember God loves you and if you need to talk to someone call your mentor or a fellow Christian for encouragement. Remember the only thing that matters is staying connected to God's Kingdom! Don't let what people say or how they treat you discourage you!

There is so much more to learn, like Bishop Christian teaches," Be a lifetime student of Jesus Christ!"

I pray this book blessed you and congratulations on your decision to be a part of the Kingdom of God!

SPECIAL THANKS!

I want to thank God, His son Jesus Christ and the Holy Spirit for never leaving me or forsaking me!

Specials Thanks to Bishop Christian, 1ˢᵗ Lady Christian, 1ˢᵗ Lady Hayes for your time, commitment and the word of God you have rightly divided in my life that has prepared me for such a time as this.

Thanks to my mother, Patricia Jones and my son, Darrell Crawford for loving me through it all!

Thanks to my best friends Ms. Bonita Warren & Mrs. Kristin Thomas for always being my friend regardless of the season. God bless you ladies for your encouragement and love!

Thanks to all the leaders and ministers that have encouraged me through the word of God. Thanks to all my friends, associates and especially my church family at Bountiful Blessings that have loved me and prayed me through so much in a short amount of time!

God bless you all for showing me Christian love!

Thank you!

Tara M. Jones